MORE THAN JUST

Poetry

MORE THAN JUST

Poetry

INSIGHT FOR OVERCOMING OBSTACLES

YUMICA P. THOMPSON

PROSE GOALS PUBLISHING
WASHINGTON, D.C.

MORE THAN JUST POETRY: INSIGHT
FOR OVERCOMING OBSTACLES

This is a work of non-fiction. All poems in this book are original works
of the author. Any similarities to other works are coincidental.

MORE THAN JUST POETRY: INSIGHT
FOR OVERCOMING OBSTACLES
© 2020 Yumica P. Thompson

Paperback ISBN-13: 978-0-578-79599-7

Published by Prose Goals Publishing
Washington, D.C.

Printed in the United States of America
First Edition November 2020

Design: Make Your Mark Publishing Solutions
Editing: Make Your Mark Publishing Solutions
Cover Art: Larenai Swann

Contents

Acknowledgements

I would like to acknowledge the following:

God—There is no me without you. You put promise on the inside of me before the day I was born. Thank you for allowing me time to cultivate my gifts. You are my always. Always loving me. Always giving me. Always ordering my steps. Always protecting me. I honor you and give all glory and praise to you now and forever!

Brenda & Lewis Thompson—You are phenomenal parents who have always believed in me. You have kept me on the straight and narrow. Guided me in my darkest days. You have equipped me with the tools that I needed to overcome difficulties. You are my biggest cheerleaders. Your strength, prayers, and understanding make you amazing and I love you!

LaTonya & Jaron Hickman—My sister and brother-in-love, I thank you for always being honest, supportive, and present. Thank you for showing up and being a part of every occasion. We have had amazing conversations and laughs. The love that you give to me, your niece, and nephew is a gift. But one of the things that impresses me most is how selfless you both are. Hugs to you both!

Paul Waldron, Sr.—I cherish our talks, and I thank you for sending me daily prayers. Your prayers help keep me grounded. I appreciate you. Always have and I always will.

Rev. Alfreda Smith—You watched me grow up and always saw something special in me. We have shared many talks honoring God. Your presence always brings joy. You are an atmosphere changer. I love you and thank God for your prayers, your wisdom, and your gift of giving. You give more than flowers. You give joy! You give happiness! You give hope!

Donnita Fowler—Whenever you have the chance to remind me of my gifts—you do. Each time I would start talking about my dream of becoming a poet, you would listen. When I would become stagnant or inactive, you told me the truth. You, like my sister, never gave up on this project. You never doubted that my dream would become a reality. I am grateful for your presence in my life. When best friends become sisters become published authors. That is us. Cheers!

Oscar Hawkins—We are cousins who grew up like brother and sister. I have learned so many things by watching you and your success. You have always believed in me. Even when I sing off-key, you've got my back. I thank you for all you do and have done for me!

Brenda Swann—I will forever appreciate your love and support. You believed in my dream of publishing my book years ago, and have shown me that same support even now. I thank you for never judging me and for always knowing deep down that I would get to the finish line.

Last but not least:

Larenai & John Swann, Jaron II & Christopher Hickman—Thank you for believing that I could do this. You knew the importance of this project and allowed me the space and time to put my thoughts on paper. I could not have asked for better children and nephews. I love you all! Follow your dreams and never give up.

Daryl D. Johnson—I appreciate the friendship we have. Thank you for believing in me. You are loved and always will be.

My Beta Readers—You know who you are. I thank you for being a part of my journey and for providing me with honest and helpful feedback. You are appreciated beyond measure.

Dedication

This book is dedicated to every person who has ever been through trauma, loss, heartache, depression, and stress. I salute you!

Introduction

There are so many days that I would sit with my thoughts and emotions, thinking to myself, how will I recover? Why do the things I want slip away? Is there a human love that will come for me one day? Why is it that sin feels just as amazing as forgiveness? Is being alone a blessing or a curse? Why do I allow hurts to get worse?

The words in my book will awaken your emotional side and disturb your pride, giving you something real to feel and think about. Only one poem in this book is a true story. Will you be able to emotionally connect to my regret?

Let me introduce myself:

I am Yumica Thompson. Born and raised in Southeast D.C. I have two amazing and well-rounded children (if I do say so myself), a super supportive and inspiring sister and brother-in-love, two loving and smart nephews, and a talented and creative best friend. Although I was born into a situation-ship—my parents met in high school and married years later—they have the longest relationship that I have known. My parents are love in motion.

I graduated from Eastern Senior High School in 1995. From a very young age, poetry lived in me. While taking classes at The University of the District of Columbia, I lost one of my closest friends (RIP Abraham Kabede), and I decided college was not going to carry me to my destiny. I was broken, and I began to seek employment in retail, became a security officer, concierge, and worked as an administrative assistant, all to put food on my table. Through these experiences, I realized nothing satisfied me as much as words, wisdom, and time.

Words give me healing. Wisdom gives me insight. Time creates space for my passion and purpose.

The poems, insight, self-reflection, and prayers in this book have been written purposefully and intentionally to help create an intimate space for healing, forgiveness, and a new perspective on love (or a friendly reminder), to make it easier to move past the obstacles of life experiences and trauma.

All subject matters touch my heart, and I hope they will touch yours too.

My poems are inspired by personal experiences and world events.

Please enjoy!

#thejoyofpartnership

The joy of partnership is…
Lots of laughter during holidays, or trying to get through a hardship's maze.
It's giving friendly reminders or the covering of a scar.
It's listening to your spouse sing off-key when their favorite song is playing in the car.
It's eating breakfast sometimes slightly before midnight.
It's not giving up on each other the calm after the fight.
It's comforting and supporting when events in your day cause you to cry.
It's taking your word at face value because on you they can rely.
It's a look that only your partner gives to you.
It's financially supporting the dreams they choose to pursue.
It's apologizing even when you know they're not right.
It's about compromising to avoid a potential fight.
It's about clapping back for each other when under attack.
It's about confidence in the one you love having your back.

It realizes God first, then family and friends.

It's about recognizing that true love stories never end!

It's about sound advice and sharing.

It's about being happy with the one you married.

It's about being free to express yourself without prejudice or shame.

It's about loving them even though your love language isn't always the same.

It's about choosing to love someone when life appears fuzzy, hazy, and lazy…

It's about loving them even though they may make you crazy.

It's about giving your partner space and room to create.

It's about loving unconditionally, even when neither can relate.

Because the joy of partnership is fate…

#thejoyofpartnership

INSIGHT

When love is unconditional, it will grow. It truly takes two to communicate. Two to forgive. Two to accept. Two to move past regret. For many this type of love is unknown. Unconditional love towards them is seldom shown. But never love someone out of convenience. Love them because you mean it.

There is no greater love than that of John 3:16. "For God so loved the world that he gave his only begotten son, and whosoever believes in him shall not perish but have everlasting life."

REFLECTION

- Have you been in love?
- Did you listen and respect their concerns?
- Did you build them up or did you tear them down?
- If you answered yes to the first question, are they still around?

PRAYER

Dear God, thank you for loving us without condition. Thank you for allowing us the free will to choose what we think is best for us. Please show your love for this reader over and over again as it is written, until they know that there is no greater love for them than yours. A man or woman's love is temporary. But your love for us, Lord, endures forever. Amen.
(Jeremiah 31:3)

A Woman's Tears

When a woman sheds tears
She is thinking and reflecting
She is redirecting her fretting
And looking forward to her blessings

Her tears are years loved
Years lost; tears burned
And years learned

Her tears are confirmation that fear no longer holds over her a
power or need for concern
Her tears will emotionally disconnect from past tenses
Her tears no longer need fences

Through her tears a newborn freedom she seeks

A freedom attached to God's word, God's power, God's sheep

Each tear is like fresh rain washing over a dirty city

A rain that transforms dirty and gritty to sparkling and pretty.

The tears of a woman will take her from sad to mad to hopeful
and glad

Each tear drop is a drop that will stop her life's inconsistencies
and unproven mysteries

They will stop a hand hitting her face as she begins to walk in
God's grace

They will stop a new call to a cop

They will cause her knees to drop

Her curls from falling and
Her life from stalling

When her tears no longer fall
When she barely answers your call
Her drops become dry
And she finds no reason to cry

Just know that her tears don't lie
And that last cry is goodbye

A Woman's Tears

INSIGHT

A woman's tears will spiritually cleanse her. Help her kick her fears to the curb, and allow her to move on. Her tears create a space for the Holy Spirit to operate freely within her so that her love, dreams, and desires can be moved from the realm of toxic blame and shame, to declaration and domain. There is power in the tears of a woman. And just because a woman is able to move on doesn't mean that she will never cry again.

REFLECTION

- What continues to hurt you that you need to cry about?
- Are you ready to accept your part in your disappointment?
- Do you believe your tears will make room for your joy?

PRAYER

Heavenly Father, remove anything and anyone from this reader that causes them hurt, anger, and pain. Let the tears that fall from their eyes be tears of joy. Holy Spirit, clear their path and make your presence known. Amen.
(Psalm 34:17)

Accepting Me

I woke up
Smiling different
Feeling different
Listening different
Seeing different
The beat of my heart was once faint in sound to me
Because I couldn't hear it from the hurt inside of me
My smile was up only when others were in my sight
There were moments that I've cried throughout an entire night
Do you feel me?
I am a daughter, a single mother, an on-and-off-again girlfriend,
a baby momma, a niece

God rescue me…! I need some peace!

But today I smile because I AM HAPPY
I feel different because God dwells in me

I listen different because I care
I see different because at myself I stare
I no longer ache for love unavailable
I no longer allow another sad love song
from the men who string me along and then,
poof, they're gone

I am a daughter, a single mother, a warrior
A work in progress... One of God's best

Accepting me for me because I'm blessed!

Accepting Me

INSIGHT

It takes a great amount of courage to let go of the negative attachments that other people put upon you. Changing the words that you speak over yourself and in your life diminishes every ugly word and title someone gives you. The power of positivity jumpstarts your self-esteem, and the inner beauty you sometimes hide becomes live and in living color.

REFLECTION

- When you look at yourself, what is it you see?
- What are the things that you are ready to embrace?
- What are the things you see that you are ready to change?

PRAYER

Thank you, Lord, for allowing the reader to see themselves in a new light. Please give them divine sight that will keep them grounded in you. Let their light never dim, even when they hear negative words about themselves. Remind them, Lord, that they are wonderfully made in your image. Amen.
(2 Corinthians 5:17)

Bastard Boy!

You put it to me
I took it

I walked a straight line
You walked crooked

I fed you love
You were never starved

You fed me lies
My emotions scarred

You felt me up
I liked it

You put me first
You took a risk

Then suddenly you put it to me like this:
I never meant for you to see that kiss
It was wrong for me to ice her wrist
The smell between her legs made me beg
I wouldn't miss you if you were dead
I took away about five years of your time
You should've introduced me to nickels, not dimes
You, my friend, are fine… but love is blind and I don't apologize

Bastard Boy!

INSIGHT

How many people have loved you until they met someone else, then loved them too? The betrayal is more than complicated. It will leave you jaded. So how do you deal with this? Do you pretend it never happened? Or do you pray your heartache away? Remember when you decide to cheat on other people you end up cheating yourself.

Know that when you begin to kneel and pray, Jesus will pick up the pieces of your despair.

REFLECTION

- Have you ever cheated on someone? How did that make you feel? Have you ever been cheated on?
- Did you leave or did you stay?
- What tied/ties you to people who disappoint you?
- Did/do you have a plan to walk away?

PRAYER

Father God, give this reader the courage to walk away from people and things who no longer serve a purpose in their life. Help them to detach from things that have grown familiar. Give them the desire to keep you first and let nothing separate their love from you. Amen.

(Psalm 1:1)

Born Again

Caught up... Captured.
Can't see... Can't breathe.
Worried... Scared.
Help me...! Help Me!
I'm Dying.

My future has slipped.
It's un-gripping.
My past taunts me and haunts me.
My present does not forewarn me.
The enemy has taken over.

My skeleton is shelter for my inner demon
Can't free myself!

REBIRTH... REBORN
These are the words that echo in my mind.

I'm confused.
I repeat them over and over again.
Can't figure out the message.
Can't figure out the lie beneath the heat that journeys me.

I'm overheated.
But I no longer sweat.
My fears take over my pains... I'm scared!
I am being held hostage.
My awareness deepens.
I want out of this entrapment.

I panic... I pray... nothing happens.
I plead... I cry... nothing happens.

I feel lonely and abandoned.
These words continue to fill the space left in my memory.

REBORN... REBIRTH

These words are still unclear.
I restlessly think.
I start to remember.

Time—1985
I was fourteen and felt alive.
Went to church with Aunt Sue and Uncle Homer.
Pastor was talking about baptism and being saved.
I chuckled to myself because, to me, it sounded like foolishness.
I was way too grown at that time for my age, filled with cluelessness,
And being saved just wasn't on my to-do list.

There were folk dancing, prancing, and fainting.
They called it catching the Holy Ghost.
I just stood frozen like a security guard at their post.

Now I realize the message of those words.
I needed to let my old ways die to give birth to anew.
Which is the ultimate sacrifice that Christians yearn and pursue.

At that moment I opened my heart and let my Savior in.
The stronghold was released along with my error and sin.
If I had known then what I know now.
I would have gotten saved long ago.
Nowadays, not only does my light shine… It glows.

Grateful on that night when I felt alone and torn,
That night I chose Jesus and now I'm reborn.

Born Again

INSIGHT

When we are younger, it is not always easy to understand the importance of salvation, or what it even means. Oftentimes younger people feel dragged to church rather than being invited. It can be quite an overwhelming experience. And instead of running to God's house, you tend to run closer to sin. Then one day you remember those good old days at church. And it happens—you accept Jesus as your Lord and Savior. Your flesh dies so that the spirit in you may rise. You experience transformation and conversion. An event that makes you feel like you died is the same event that makes you feel alive.

REFLECTION

- Have you been baptized? If so, do you remember how that made you feel?
- When was the last time you performed a flesh check?
- How do you keep your spirit aligned with God's will?

PRAYER

Gracious and wonderful Father, I pray that the reader who is reading this and is not saved has a heart change and invites you into their lives. I pray they accept Jesus Christ as their Lord and Savior. I pray they fall in love with you and your Word. Lord, give them the desire to repent. The desire to confess. The desire to ask you for forgiveness. And the desire to testify in your name. Amen.

(Romans 10:9-10)

Breaking Chains of Shame

We do things in life that don't always align with our beliefs, but instead align with our circumstances.

We give up things that are important because of doubt, worry, and fear!

We carry around the unhappiness of our decision in our heart, our flesh, our soul.

It makes us tender and eager to reject the idea that love can be real because of what we did and what we hid.

Ya see… shame drains you and attaches itself to words like **HATE**, **UNWORTHY**, **LONELY**.

Your shame meets you in your sleep and taunts you. It destroys your inner peace and ages you. You begin to appear fragile, weak, empty.

Your silence traps your spirit.

You cry. You cry. YOU CRY!

No one hears you or sees you because you've allowed your shame to make you invisible.

Darkness seeks you out! You fight it. It's strong.

Darkness sweet-talks you so that you become emotionally detached from healing. From feeling. From loving.

You are in a constant battle. No one knows but you what you did or why.

No one sees you're hurting, because your smile has become a permanent lie to shield your pain from nosy folk whose opinions are just that.

Gossip comes alive!

They plan to tell your story but not learn the lesson. Gossipers plan to tell your story without showing concern. Gossipers plan to tell your story without your permission. Funny thing about when they tell "your" story—people listen.

Gossip entertains them!

But you are stronger than you give yourself credit for!

As a still night comes preparing for the sun, you hear a whisper! Your shame shatters. Your tears flow! You surrender all.

At that moment, you know all you've done has been forgiven.

The Lord reveals that he died for you and paid a hefty price for your sin.

He wipes your tears and erases your fears and loves you. You are surrounded with light, with hope, with love.

Your silence is now replaced with synonyms and metaphors. Your story written. Your truth revealed!

But are you free?

Your words have power!

Can you see?

Your story belongs to you!

Are you healed?

Only God knows what your truth will do!

In this life… it is imperative to know that one can only remain sane by breaking chains of shame.

And like butterflies in clear blue skies
Jesus gives you power to RISE!

By resting assured in your Savior's eternal promises.

Breaking Chains of Shame

INSIGHT

Shame, lies, and dirty little secrets will steal away the joys that God has given to you. The only way to free yourself is to confess, repent, forgive, and operate in God's spirit and in His truth. Don't let past mistakes torture you or keep you from progressing. Some pains are lessons, while others are blessings. But if you do not set yourself free, true joy in your life will never be. The choice is yours. Deliverance can be your reality. It is never too late to separate yourself from sin.

REFLECTION

- What mistake or transgression possesses your mind?
- Does this thing make you weak, causing you to lose sleep?
- Have you forgiven yourself?

PRAYER

Heavenly Father, the enemy comes to steal, kill, and destroy us. Help the reader bind up on earth and in heaven the enemy's tactics, poison, and deceit. Renew their minds daily, Lord, and may you continue to be their help and their strength. Amen. (Psalm 28:7-8)

Buried Alive

Captured… Can't get out
The air is thin… I'm faint
My pulse is weak… I'm desperate
No one hears me or sees me

It all started when I refused to obey
Got tired of black eyes and foolish lies
Outgrew my childhood to become grown
He treated me like a child
One he'd grown to own

Fix my supper
Wash my feet
Comb my hair
Scrub my floor
Wash my tub

Get me a beer
And a full-body rub

So many wants and commands
Not to mention sex every night
And the first time I said no
He planted a full-body blow

Sure, there were yells and tears
Nothing compares to the torture over the years

I feared outside
I feared inside, too
I feared my own shadow
You would fear the same
If you were beaten
BLACK and BLUE

Life became pretty miserable for me
Even when I was sick
That SOB beat me with a stick

He always told me that I could never leave
Said he'd kill me if I tried

I got away for six months
And when he found me
I found his fist in my side
Along with his broken heart
And his broken pride

The only man I ever loved went and dug my grave
He placed my body inside the dirt
Said next time maybe I'd behave

Grief and regret filled my heart
As the weight of the dirt hit my face
It was even harder for me to feel
those worms crawling around my waist

I had no way out
All I could do was cry
My fate had come to its final end
It was time for me to die

Ladies and gents, when you meet a friend
Please follow the warning signs
Because love is only special
When love isn't blind

I took one last breath
And angels greeted me
I had no peace on earth
But heaven awaited me

Buried Alive

INSIGHT

Love will NEVER hurt you. Love will never attack you or your character. Love will never dig you a grave! Don't be afraid to test someone's spirit. Don't be afraid to disconnect from anybody who lashes out at you, disrespects you, humiliates you, taunts you, drags your name in the mud, shows envy, or stabs you in the back. God has written instructions to help us avoid those disguised as righteous, but sent to rearrange our lives with hate, abuse, lies, and torment. Reading the Word of God will prepare you for every battle, and having faith in God will win every fight.

REFLECTION

- Have you ever trusted someone who turned out to be your worst enemy?
- If so, how did you break ties with that person?
- Have you ever been physically abused?
- If so, how did it end, and have you been able to forgive?

PRAYER

Dear God, cover the abused in the mighty name of Jesus. Erase their worries, fear, and shame. Show the reader who has faced or is facing domestic trauma that you are bigger. Create a space for them to get away, Lord God. Let them escape to a new way of living. Give them peace, and in return, let them shower you with thanksgiving and praise. Amen.
(2Timothy 3:1-8)

Change

You stay
You breathe
You stay
You consume
You stay
You groom
You stay
You lay
You stay
You sleep
You stay
You take
You stay
You stay
And you stay
But not once have you paid a bill

I've been trying to tell you thirty ways that you don't get thirty
days
You've been:
Enlightened
Valued
Involved
Cared for
Tolerated
Enjoyed
Deleted

#evicted

Change

INSIGHT

Oftentimes we allow things in our life to linger way past the expiration date. We give up our power to be heard. We settle for being settled. We believe that God will fix it. We try over and over again to make sense out of a senseless situation. We cave because loneliness scares us more than death. We put up with disappointment.

Never allow another person who has not made a commitment to you to take hold of your possessions or offer you direction. For anything to work cohesively in your life, you must seek God's guidance and approval. God will add to your life what you need, and he will assist in the removal of what you don't. Trust God in all your endeavors if you want your life to be better.

REFLECTION

- What or who are you holding on to that no longer serves a purpose in your life?
- Is it easy for you to make decisions?
- Are you ready to say goodbye and be okay?
- While you make changes to clear your path, are you willing to change yourself?

PRAYER

Lord God, please help the reader recognize when it's time to let go of underserving relationships. Remind them there is a

season for everything. Equip them with discernment, and let no weapon formed against them prosper. Amen.
(Ecclesiastes 3:6)

Choose Wisely

Sex cannot fix emotional brokenness.
Being in tune with God is a must.
Happiness starts with you.
Financial stability and security are important.
Apologies mean nothing if the intent is the same.
When people leave, never open that door again.
Nobody deserves distance with conditions.
Control works when you're emotionally down.
A person cannot choose to leave and to stay around.
Mistreated people are usually givers.
Don't let your light dim or your sincerity wither.
Some people only care about their problems.
But will you continue to eat at the same table with them
Or will you starve them?

Choose Wisely

INSIGHT

Why is it that people start out one way and end up another? A person can be your solution or your problem. Do you desire the company of a murderer, a thief, or a liar? Only you can choose your desires. Start by listing your dos and don'ts, or won't and wants. Don't give permission to people who mistreat you. It is okay to unlove and disconnect from anything that brings you sadness, stress, or pain.

REFLECTION

- Do people in your life know upfront that they must treat you the way they want to be treated?
- How do you manage disrespect?
- Is the company you keep a liability or a benefit?
- What steps have you taken to make wise choices?

PRAYER

Most gracious Father, please let the reader be careful who they sleep with, drink with, or eat with. Help them understand that when people show us who they are, we should believe them. Give them Holy Ghost power to choose you, Father, and your love, above anyone or anything. Amen.

(1 Corinthians 5:11)

Deadbeat Dad

Dear deadbeat dads,

To walk away after years of lovemaking that produced creations of a me and a you is plain foul.

How can one abandon their children… their child?

No excuses for you!

Because mommas have the same nothing as you, but still make do.

They strategize and recognize that failing to plan was a mistake, but planning to fail again and again is a habit to break.

Any momma expects for a man to stay…

A man who she has loved, forgiven, respected, lived with.
A man who she believed and believed in.
A man who was not perfect, but born to win.
A man she thought was her friend.

So, for every occasion you've missed

Their first tooth
First walk
First graduation
Their first car and first date

Your mistake!

Stop dating and creating life with women you don't love.

Deadbeat Dad

INSIGHT

Abandonment has become a universal sore spot for children and adults across the world. Abandoned children become abandoned adults. It is very important to speak life and healing over this type of hurt. If the pain from this type of absence is not addressed, it will become one of the heaviest bags someone can carry into present and future relationships. And dads are not the only ones who leave their children hanging, but there are an overwhelming number of dads who have made it easier to call them out for it.

REFLECTION

- Do you know the pain of abandonment?
- Are you taking steps to heal from it?
- Can you forgive your offender?

PRAYER

My Father, who art in heaven, please release the reader from the pain of abandonment. You are the beginning and the end. Alpha and Omega. And you promise to never leave or forsake us. Please stick close to them, Lord. I pray they learn to put their trust and confidence in you. For you are a strong tower, a rock in sinking sand, the lily of the valley, the Great I AM. And if you healed this type of pain before, surely you can do it again according to your will. Amen.
(Psalm 27:10)

Death

Death may stop sadness
Death may stop hurt and pain
But death won't heal your lies or forgive your shame

Death won't cuddle you or kiss you goodnight.

Death is neither wrong nor right.

Death is
Death will be
Death has been

Death may be your only friend.

Death strokes your soul and prepares you for your fate.

Death gives you a second chance to repent. To love. To relate.

Death is powerful, bold, and has an unfamiliar scent.

Death collects your time like a landlord collects your rent.

Death is surely to come like the first of each month. Death is neutral, faithful, prompt.

Death is a must
Death is a guarantee
Death is a will-be

You cannot run from it
Hide from it
Escape it
Reject it
Fake it
or
Delay it

The truth is:

Death is the best peace and sleep
It allows you to slumber deep
Death stops time, sickness, and sorrow
It makes people forget what you've borrowed

Death covers you like a blanket.
It allows you to see things you need to see.
Death is a sunny day on a stormy night.
Death is your birthright.
Now, goodnight. Sleep tight.
Because death is…

Death

INSIGHT

Death is inevitable, yet it is universally feared. It is like solving for x in an algebraic equation. Things that are unknown tend to cause extreme worry or anxiety. But God gives us hope even in death. His promise of eternal life is intended for us to know that death is not our end. Believing this is paramount to your faith and discipleship.

REFLECTION

- How old were you when you discovered the true meaning of death?
- Did this information ease your anxiety?
- When was the last time you shared God's promise of eternal life with someone else?
- Have you prepared your loved ones for your wishes when death knocks at your door?

PRAYER

Almighty God, please bring comfort to the reader, giving to them peace that death is also destination. It is the end of carnal life, and the beginning to a new life prepared for them to honor and to serve you, Lord, in your Kingdom. I pray that the thought of death steals joy from their mind no more. Instead let them rejoice knowing that what is yet to come is blessed by your love, power, and authority. Amen.
(John 11:25-26)

Drained

Here we go again, another request from you, you, and you…
If it is not about help with your bills or advice on your thrills
Then it's every question that starts with "will."
Like:
Will you buy my food?
Will you pick up my kids?
Will you go to the store?
Will you give me a little more?
But when I am tapped out, who is there for me?
Because I don't see you, you, you, or you around to improve my sanity.
Each request, whether large or small, takes my energy from twenty to ten
The more I do for you, you, and you
The less I want to remain your friend
Ya see, for relationships to elevate
Each person has to reciprocate

But when I give and give and give
And all you do is take
Then it is time to get on my knees and pray
that selfish and one-sided relationships fade away

No longer am I a one-stop shop for all your needs

Personally, and professionally, when I learned to say "no,"
I was freed.

When giving you takes away from me, I am giving you permission to use me

And I'd rather say "no" to you to prevent you from losing me.

 *Drained*

INSIGHT

Be careful not to allow people pleasing to become a sin. Being available for someone every time they are in need will rob you of your energy. Not to mention that God is a jealous God. There should be nothing or no one placed above him. When you are at the beck and call of people, and they are not at your beck, not only does this qualify as a one-sided relationship, but it gives them power to guilt you. Learning it is okay to say no and still be loved is a key component to your mental and emotional growth. Get off the people pleasing merry-go-round. Begin living your life in peace and balance.

REFLECTION

- If you are a people pleaser, what frightens you about saying no?
- How often do people say no to you? Do you think it's fair?
- Will you continue allowing others to drain you?
- How do you plan to make a change?

PRAYER

In the mighty name of Jesus, God, I ask that the reader finds confidence in you. That they begin evaluating their relationships, as well as do a self-check. Lord, remove anyone from their lives who takes offense to their growth. Let their relationships be in balance by giving and receiving without bribes, plots, or schemes behind it. Lord God, remind the reader that

no one can out-give you. Heighten their discernment, Lord. Let them seek your wisdom in all their decisions to prevent them from being used and drained by the enemy (sometimes known as family or friends). Amen.
(Ephesians 5:15-17)

For It Is Well

There's nothing like the love between a mother and her child
There is nothing sweeter than a sibling's hug, kiss, and smile
There's nothing stronger than a father's commitment and bond
Yet these are all things that will be missed when it's all said and done.

An uncle's helping hand or a grandmother's wish
Cousins laughing and memories bliss
Godparents cheering for the family to win
Friendships that remained loyal to the very end.

It's time for the living to seek eternal life and confess
For there is hope and peace in eternal rest.
Let's not dwell in sadness or in sorrow
For life doesn't promise us a definite tomorrow.
If our loved ones could share with us one last thing
It would be to enjoy life and the fun times it'll bring.

Though it hurts that loved ones have gone on
and that we are left
I assure you that Jesus takes his very best!

And every time you hear the ringing of a bell
Think of a favorite memory and smile...
For it is well!

For It Is Well

INSIGHT

You can be here today and gone tomorrow. Never take the time spent with your family and friends for granted. Be sure to make lasting memories. Memories are what is left to help you cope with grief and move on. And don't shy away from the people who love you when their transition is near. Instead, look them in the eyes and tell them you love them. Hold their hand and sing to them their favorite song. Showing your support is more than just stopping past to visit—it is being present with them in their final moments.

REFLECTION

- Is there a friend or loved one you are ignoring out of fear of losing them?
- Are you willing to be delivered from that fear so you can show them your support?
- It is never too late to give people their flowers while they are alive. Are you willing to reach out and do this for someone you love?

PRAYER

Our Father, who art in heaven, hallowed be thy name—bring comfort and understanding to the reader that all things are done according to your perfect will. Assure them, Lord, that the memories they hold near and dear to their hearts will get them through this process. Keep their minds sound, Lord, and let them find healing in your Word as it is written, and in time let them declare that it is well. Amen.

(John 14:1-3)

Free

I can't love you and not trust you at the same time.

I'm Free!

You may be telling the truth, but your past taught me you're lying.

I'm Free!

I can't feel hope and hate in the same breath.

I'm Free!

I can't feel you're here for me when distance knows you best.

I'm Free!

I can't wipe my soul of memories old, and I can't see a future with you stamped sold.

I'm Free!

The life I live is neither here nor there.

I'm Free!

No matter how many times you say that you care.

I'm Free!

No.Longer.A.Slave.To.Your.Sin.

Free

INSIGHT

You've heard it before: when people show you who they are, you should believe it. Stop allowing people space to occupy your mind with falsehoods. Their actions towards you should be a deterrent or an attraction. Start applying wisdom and discernment in your life. Armor up! It takes but a little while for a person to catch a slave, but it takes years for a slave to be separated from that person. Don't let this be you.

REFLECTION

- How do you determine who should stay in your life and who should go?
- Do you sit on the same porch as misery?
- Is walking away from the hurt of someone simple, or does it require planning?
- Can you name anything that is more important than your sanity?

PRAYER

Father God, I pray that the reader is delivered from people who lie to them, steal their time, use them, place doubt on the inside of them, and disrespect them, all while claiming to love them. Loose them from this bondage, Lord. Free them and motivate them to testify in your name. Amen.
(John 8:34)

Freed

I have cried so many tears that I found myself
drowning and sinking into a despaired state.

No one knows my struggles, because from my toes
to my waist to my face... my sadness is well hidden.

While my inner self is in hiding.
I feel unchallenged and unsatisfied.

And when you lied... I cried.

But when you died...

I realized that my hopes, dreams, and faith
were put into the wrong man.

I felt I needed you...

I yearned for you, and at the end,
I mourned you.

My breaths are trapped… caught up… contained.
The loss of your life has me feeling insane.

Then through my dreams, I have an encounter.
It was overwhelming, spiritual, and freeing!

Jesus touched my hand… I cried!
I asked him to help me and heal me.

For I knew inside my heart…
That satan was trying to steal me.

My Lord said, "Child, you must believe to be freed."
I felt stuck!
Jesus knew that my feelings for him were not 100%.

From that moment on I opened my heart and my mouth to
confess… to repent
From the really bad to the mild, I spoke of things from the then
to the now…
And from when I was a child.

I told it all… and held nothing back.
I was vulnerable and emotional.
I woke up feeling anew.
My head was clear, my tears were joyous,
And I even had a smile.

My mind had no doubts… Jesus saved me last night in my sleep. I am no longer haunted by demons or afraid to speak truth into this world.

I was reborn…! To give others the gift that my savior had given me.

THE KNOWLEDGE AND LOVE TO BE FREE!

Freed

INSIGHT

When grief knocks at your door and overwhelms you, it is hard to imagine living without the one you loved. Grief will take you on a roller coaster ride by locking you inside. It is so powerful! You cannot run. You cannot hide. But you can respond accordingly by calling on Jesus so the enemy can flee. And before you know it, the memories that broke you down will now make your heart smile.

REFLECTION

- Have you experienced grief to a point of depression?
- Which three people were there for you?
- Have you thanked them?

PRAYER

Dear God, I lift in prayer the reader who is stricken by grief and finds themselves stuck. Free them, Lord! Comfort them. Lift their heart-aching pain and depression. Fill them with hope and surround them in your light, hope, and love. Amen. (John 16:22)

Getting High

At times I feel like I'm floating
I feel like helium has been inserted into my body
I'm so high… I want to wake
Then I realize I am not dreaming

The high is so intense
My blood rushes
My salivary glands leak
My mood changes from solemn to freak

I encounter rainbows on my trip
I am flying higher than a kite
Nothing feels wrong when you're high
Just lots of time passing by

Then one sound astounds me
It's the sound of an infant in her crib

She reeks of spoiled milk
And has on a day-old bib

My body is transforming
I now feel agony and pain
Please, somebody help me
For I need another shot in my vein

I realize that baby with the brown eyes is my own
Though she's here with me, I know she feels alone
But all I want or need is the magic solution that pollutes my
brain
That magic solution that sends sensations through my vein

I want to be high

I want to ride the ocean waves
until I crash and cave

Some get high to get by
I get high just to get high

Then again, let me really tell you why

I was the one who always made honor roll
Had straight A's until grade 11
Met my first boyfriend, Kevin
Yes, he was a little frisky
And some of our behavior was risky
But I felt butterflies every time he kissed me

I lost my first child when I was with him

I was the coat hanger wrangler
I sat in the bathroom devastated
Just devastated

I was hooked and baited by almost every man I dated

But there was nobody like Jimmy
My favorite words to him were gimme, gimme, gimme
Jimmy was the one who introduced me to bud at the club
Then we would have orgies for the horny
And laugh at jokes that were corny

My momma used to warn me
About the secrets of life that could drain energy from a dried
bone
I'd listen sometimes
and other times I'd suck my teeth and moan
Now I'm grown with a baby of my own... a car... and a home

I felt like going to work was work
I made enough money as a supply clerk
But the weekend was my time to shine
And getting high to get by just wasn't my rhyme

The truth is I get high because getting high helps my HIV/AIDS
The things we do when we're young catches up to us in old age
And after five abortions I had to have my last child
Getting high and sex parties still didn't slow me down

Just know that If I was in my right mind
I would never put myself in a position to hurt an unborn kid

Unfortunately, life consequences make you do things you wish
you never did

And by the way, my baby did not catch the disease
Thought I'd let y'all know that to put y'all's mind at ease

But every night I'm sober I repeat this prayer over and over

Now I lay me down to sleep
My body hurts and my bones are weak
Lord, protect me tonight while I sleep
And forgive me for promises I failed to keep

Guide each step that my daughter takes
And while I sleep in the bed I make
Spare my soul of the burning lake
In Jesus' name, Amen

Ya see, getting high to get by is a way to cope
But life is not worth living if there is no hope

May God bless you

Getting High

INSIGHT

Life will happen. People will disappoint you. Children will test your patience. Your job may not appreciate you. Your spouse may stop noticing you. Your church may not always feel like a place where you belong. Your friends may not always understand you or act friendly towards you. You and your sibling(s) may be in conflict. Your parents may not operate in what is considered tradition. You may get tired. Your soul may weaken. Your mind might turn on you, and your heart may hold on to and host confusion… Oh, but there is a way out of life's frustrations, loneliness, abuse, and hopelessness. God provides provision and a solution to our every problem. But you have to decide to be on one accord with God. When you are not on one accord with him, you create discord in your life. If you are not careful, you will find substances as a way of escape.

REFLECTION

- Have you ever used drugs or alcohol as a way of avoiding your pain?
- How did it make you feel? And did it change your personality or lifestyle?
- What steps did you take to become free of your habit?

PRAYER

Dear God, we all have things that try to afflict us, hold us back, hurt us, misuse us, depress us, or hold us captive. The enemy is very clever, but if we do not surrender to worldly pleasures or deceit, the enemy will hold no power. If we call on the mighty name of Jesus, the enemy will hold no power. If we trust in you, Lord… the enemy will hold no power. If we have faith the size of a mustard seed, the enemy will hold no power. God, I thank you for being a God of second chances. I thank you for being a light in the darkness. I thank you for your rescue! And I pray that the reader who struggles with substance abuse, or who puts anything and anyone before You in their lives, has a full conversion turning their life completely around. Comfort them when they want to return to what is familiar. Be their power and their strength, Lord, until they are filled. And anything that causes them hurt, agony, or distraction, remove it from their midst immediately. In Jesus' name, Amen.

(Corinthians 15:33)

Growing Up

Growing up all I heard was
LAZY, wake up
FATTY, stop eating
NAPPY ROOTZ, comb your hair
UGLY, wash your face
SLUT, go upstairs
HEIFER, be quiet

But the words that hurt the most were "BITCH how could you
do this to me?"

Keep in mind I was a virgin before the crime
My momma's hands would put knots on my face
While her boyfriend would comfort my waist

At first, I was scared
Would just lie there and cry

In a monotone voice, he said he'd kill me if I tell
That was his reply

I became mentally weak
Could not eat, sleep, or think

Wanted to tell my momma

But a man who could destroy
A young girl's innocence
Surely would put her to rest

My hurt, shame, and loneliness
Helped me not to confess
Ya see
My momma mistreated me
But she also loved me best

I was always told I was the ugliest of the bunch
My grandma Sue, Uncle Butter, and cousin Cheryl's
words hurt more than eating Momma's stale lunch

But I guess that's what I get
I've always known I had beautiful eyes
But my spirit was corrupted by everyone else's lies

I never knew the freedom of thought
Not the kind of thoughts that concede you
But the kind that make you believe in you

It wasn't until rape 28, 29, 32
Sorry, y'all, I stopped counting

I just couldn't take it no more
So, I told my momma the secrets of her house
I told her the things that happened behind that locked door

The first word my momma spoke was WHORE
I said, "Momma, NO. That's not what I am.
I'm not what you think."

I was clean and now defiled
But in Momma's eyes I was an unwanted child
In my eyes I was a beautiful black child, tall and proud
I said those words and scared myself
Ya see
That was the first time I thought that way of myself
I actually said those thoughts out loud
Instead of Momma mistreating me
She should have been proud

I finally had the courage to tell somebody
What had been done to me
The truth is
If everybody from the start would have recognized my true beauty
Instead of calling me ugly
Momma's boyfriend wouldn't have gotten the chance to touch me

Well now I think highly of myself
My momma doesn't call me ugly no more
She told me that the beauty in me she always saw
She was just afraid of losing her own youth

And I was an image that stuck out in her mind
Like a sore tooth

I forgave my momma
Like I said
Momma always loved me best
Lots of therapy and love
Helped us repair the rest
By the way
Momma's boyfriend chose to take the easy route
One shot to his head and he was out

Growing Up

INSIGHT

How we start in life is not how we will finish. We will all some-day have a story to tell. The question is, will you succumb to the events in your life that bring you pain? Or will you rise above the pain and bear witness in Jesus' name? Things will happen in your life, good or bad, that are meant to awaken you, challenge you, and prepare you so that you can trust in God's unchanging hand. You do not get to choose your family, but you do get to choose how to communicate with your family, how to love your family, and to pray for them often. People will often treat or mistreat you by what they were taught and from their experiences. It doesn't make it right, but it does make it real. Growing up is not always pleasant, nor will everyone have memories of being properly cared for. Family should protect you! If this is not the case, growing your relationship with Christ will be the best decision you ever make. He will be your refuge. He will shelter you from the storm. He is your peace, and most importantly, he will give you deliverance, and he is just.

REFLECTION

- What was growing up like for you?
- Were you ever mistreated or taken advantage of?
- Who came to your rescue?

PRAYER

Lord God, the pain of our past will make us stagnant if we allow it to. It will make us believe we have no future. The pain and memories will linger in our lives until we take away their power. Lord God, help the reader take away the power of their past. Help them grow and praise your Holy name in and out of season. Help them to experience the full joy of your promises. Help them to know that what happens to us does not define who we are. Lord God, I pray the reader forgives the people who hurt them, and uses it as a tool to teach and witness to others. Protect them, Lord. Stretch them, Lord. And let no weapon formed against them prosper. Amen.

(Jeremiah 17:7)

Hands Made for Heaven

My hands don't just cook, clean, do hair,
clean wounds, massage away the troubles of your day…
MY HANDS… They PRAY!
They praise, they raise reverence on high, they wipe tears away
when I cry
MY HANDS… Aren't Shy!
They remember who, what, when, where, and why
THEY LIFT GLORY BECAUSE OF MY STORY!
My HANDS are more than what you think
They are my worship link
So, yes, my hands may clean and cheer or grab you a cold beer
But the POWER in these hands knows no fear
They will caress you with care
Bless your head of hair

Knit and stitch you a new outfit

Pray you out of a pit

High five each new strive

These Hands

My Hands

Are praise raisers, God chasers, way makers, oven bakers

They conceal scars, they carry bags, they write, they type, they open the Word,

They iron, they bathe, they cook, they fix, they prepare, they gather, they wash, they hold, they mold

These Hands

My Hands

Are purposeful and uniquely made

They remember the hardship of the slave

They remember the deep holes for my ancestors' graves

These Hands

My Hands

Will heal you, instead of stealing joy from you

They will comfort you, instead of slapping pain to your face

They will hold your hand while running the race

These Hands

My Hands

Extend Love

Not just any love, but the Love of my Father and His son Jesus

That John 3:16 love

That 1 Corinthians 13:4-5 love

That Luke 6:35 love

That Romans 12:9 love

That Mark 12:31 love

That Ephesians 4:2 love

That 1 Peter 4:8 love

That Colossians 3:14 love
That Proverbs 10:12 love
That Matthew 6:24 love
Our Hands are the beginning to winning
By opening God's Word with your hands
They help free you from sinning
These Hands
My Hands
Are not used but useful
They are destiny or demise
Start seeing your hands with new eyes
for your hands and my hands are made for heaven

Hands Made for Heaven

INSIGHT

There are so many variations of praising and glorifying God. Some people sing or dance, but there is so much reverence that you can show God through your hands, your eyes, or silent cries. What do you do daily to show your respect for God? The list of things that God does for you prior to you completely starting your day is impressive. He wakes you up, protects you from accidents that lie ahead; He gives you resources to keep a roof over your head. Please stay in God's will and see how much he operates in your life on your behalf. For without God's grace and mercy, which is sufficient, you would not exist in peace.

REFLECTION

- Is praising God a part of your worship experience?
- Is the praise you give to God your best?
- Do you give God the time in your day that he deserves?
- Going forward, will you look at your hands differently?

PRAYER

Heavenly Father, thank you for waking the reader up this morning. Thank you for allowing them to come this far in my book. Lord, we glorify your holy name on high. We promise that our praise will not be shy. Thank you, Lord, for all that you do, have done, and will do in our lives. Hallelujah! Amen. (Isaiah 25:1)

Healed by Faith

Cancer may tear at your soul…
But God remains in control!
It may thin your hair or darken your skin…
But real beauty lies within.
It may ache your body down to the bone…
But everlasting life is your true home.
It may bring nurses and doctors around…
But Jesus Christ can always be found.
Create your day beyond what your body feels.
Anticipate the day that you will be healed.
Never miss a day of prayer or supplication.
Cancel out in your mind all misinformation.
Eagerly await your whole and restorative healing.
Remember to keep Jesus Christ first no matter how you're feeling.
The creator uniquely and wonderfully made you.

There has not been a situation yet that He hasn't brought you through.

So, to the cancer that has come... the body cannot control the mind.

Friend, please appreciate every laugh, embrace every hug, and enjoy the melodies of song...

And remember that putting your faith in Jesus will never be wrong!

Christ's Anointing Nourishes, Cleans, Energizes, Restores

And by your faith and his stripes, you are healed.

Healed by Faith

INSIGHT

An unfavorable diagnosis will quickly disturb your peace. It will stir up fear, worry, and doubt. It will make you feel like there is no way out. It will rob you of sleep and give you a mindset of defeat. But God's Word gives us rest, wisdom, and strategies to overcome anything. God already knows that the enemy will plant your feet on sinking sand, but believers know that on Christ the solid rock we stand. Let everything that hath breath praise the Lord!

REFLECTION

- What diagnosis or symptoms have you had that caused you to worry?
- Are you currently going through a health scare that is distracting you from God?
- If so, how are you prepared to recover?

PRAYER

Precious Lord, please take the hand of the reader and hold it tight. If they need healing, Lord, heal them. Touch them, Lord, from the top of their heads to the soles of their feet, and bless them in a mighty way as you make them whole. Amen.
(Jeremiah 17:14)

Here's the Story

Here's the story
When you first met me
You ignored me

However, you respected me
Because I respected myself
You became interested when I shared
The pain of the cards God dealt

We shared six months of lovin' and funnin'
And not once did you mention your kids
I found that a bit weird

Your plan was to make me love you
Before discovering the truth

The truth is, I don't want the role of momma
Times however many
My own is plenty

I don't want the responsibility of another woman's drama
I was feeling you, but now I feel bad karma
What made you think I would commit
To your five kids plus my own
Which would make six

Some say I'm wrong for the way I feel
But let's keep it real
A big family I can admire
But for now, it's not my desire

Peace.

Here's the Story

INSIGHT

How often have you met someone who you became infatuated with, only to later find out that there is more to their story? Information that, if you stay with them, can and will change your life. There are certain details about who we are that should be disclosed up front. Sharing such knowledge allows the person we are attracted to the ability to decide if they would like to continue along with us. Standard information that ID us such as: name, relationship with God, how many children we have, and if we are working. If any one of these details are withheld in the beginning, do you continue being fooled? God is a God that does not lie, and He wants us connected to like-minded people. People who will not withhold the truth from us. People who will be considerate of our feelings and will not want us to compromise our morals. To avoid falling for the one who makes you love them before they share important details and intimacies about their lives… **guard your heart!** (Trust me, you will thank me for this insight—if not now, then later.)

REFLECTION

- Have you fallen for someone before knowing important facts about their lives?
- Did you continue seeing them, or did you end it?
- What questions do you ask in the beginning when meeting someone new?
- Is it time to revisit the questions you ask when forming new relationships?

PRAYER

Heavenly and Most Gracious Father, all-knowing and almighty God, the world constantly tries to fool us, manipulate us, and blindside us with lies. Lord God, please help the reader to guard their hearts and their minds and stay focused on you. Let nothing or no one put a veil on them. Allow them clear vision, and give them courage to ask open-ended questions. Protect the reader, Lord God, all the days of their life, and may they never doubt you or your direction. Amen.

(Romans 16:17-18)

I Fail Not

Another attempt failed
My heart treated as if it's replaceable
My feelings crushed because my relationship started with lust
vs friendship

I am a stronger me and he may be a stronger he
Without God first, and in the center of the way we think, act,
and converse
No wonder this relationship felt cursed

No wonder it did not move or grow
No wonder the arrow was already preset in the bow
No wonder there were lies, cheating, and deceit
No wonder every obstacle felt incomplete

To think… I thought this was it
I finally had myself a winner

To think... I fought for energy that could not deliver
To think I allowed sin to make me a sinner

Love is not about the way that we lose
Love is about the choices we choose

Will you be a benefit or a regret?
Will you be an opinion or a fact?

Another attempt did fail
But I am...

Finally
Aware
In
Love

I am Happy. I am Peace. I am Joy. I am Self-control. I am High
Self-esteem.

Simply put, I get it!

Happiness starts and ends with me... loving me.

And because of the lessons that I got

I Fail Not!

I Fail Not

INSIGHT

Don't allow fear to keep you tied to unappreciation and rejection. In relationships, there should always be something that ties two people together and allows room for growth, accountability, and responsibility. If you or your significant other feel humdrum and lack the motivation to reach common goals, then it could be a sign of disconnection. Anyone who is not tied to God and His love you should not romantically entertain. The key is understanding that unchaining yourself is not because you don't love that person—it's because YOU love YOU. Begin making notes to remind yourself that God only wants the best for you and that His love never fails.

REFLECTION

- When you met your significant other, were you afraid to ask them questions about their hopes, dreams, and goals?
- Did your relationship with that person move too fast?
- Did you check to see if their income could support the outcome of your desires?

PRAYER

Heavenly Father, teach the reader that if they put their trust in you, wisdom and discernment is at their fingertips. Teach them, Lord, that there are many wolves that dress as sheep. Help them to understand the power of their purpose. Disconnect them from stagnation and disrespect. Let them know, Lord, that your love endures forever. Every time they try again with faith the size of a mustard seed, let them know that in due time, they will be blessed with the desires of their heart according to your will. Amen.

(1 John 4:18-19)

I Matter

Tired of giving my heart without return on my investment
Tired of the older I get the more I feel desperate
Tired of loving people who refuse to see my worth
When they are incapable while still hurting from their hurts

My love is the best part of the sun's rise
It's the deep in my eyes where happiness resides
I'm the one subject that cannot be graded
And my sincerity cannot be debated
I am seen as the best challenge or worst obstacle
And sometimes I am seen as both

Having the love of a man sounds better in theory
Yet the thought of not having a man marry me is scary
It drives me crazy
It makes me weary
It mists my eyes, making them teary

Gave my heart away to men
who I no longer call friend
Their stories are a part of me
but do not define my wholeness
My love is unique and full of boldness
So, how is it that no man wants to commit to this?

I know that my best days are now
I say this and I smile
I exist now more than ever
Because I have discovered MY OWN WORTH
And I choose what to go through
Dear pain and hurt, I'm a woman of value

Because I matter to God

I am the teacher and the student
Sometimes I'm both
I am the pH balance that determines my growth

There is substance to my life

Even if never asked—will you become my…

Wisdom
Inheritance
Faith-filled
Enthusiast

I am called a lesson and a blessing
And sometimes both

I now understand who I am
And no matter the chatter
With or without that man

I matter!

 *I Matter*

INSIGHT

The most common question that single women and men get asked is, "Why aren't you married?" This question insinuates that something must be wrong with you that nobody has joined their life with yours. The world looks at your singleness and magnifies it every year that you grow older. But this is a trick of the enemy. He wants to cause loneliness, self-doubt, and low self-esteem. He wants you to feel invisible. He wants to dim your light. It is important that you focus on the love of God. Enjoy your life, and if you desire to be married, keep the faith. God promises that anything that is asked in prayer shall be received if you have faith (Matthew 21:22). And I say to you that it is far better to be single than to be tied to someone who does not believe in God or share your core values.

REFLECTION

- Have you ever felt like a third wheel when hanging out with your married friends or friends who are dating?
- How often does being single make you feel insecure?
- Are you emotionally ready to date?

PRAYER

Heavenly Father, thank you for showing favor in my life. Lord, it is an honor to be tied to your grace and your mercy. Father, give the reader a sign that where they are is where they're supposed to be. Help them not rush into the arms of the deceiver. Let them stand firm on your promises. Let their light attract light. Let their desires come to pass, Lord, according to your will. In Jesus' name. Amen.

(2 Corinthians 6:14)

I Was Surrounded

I was surrounded
They used rope and duct tape
To perform their acts of hate
They slapped me around just for fun
Broke my jaw
Cracked a rib
And bruised my lung

Then things got mental
They took turns abusing my genitals
Thought I was dead
My flesh stung all over
Doctor said my condition was rare
At my face I can't bear to stare
My speech slurred
My vision blurred
Got five different diseases

Running around in me
One tested positive for HPV

I lay alive while all that pain was inflicted
To this day none of the suspects were caught and convicted
I feel faceless and graceless
When will my memory erase this?
Though I got out alive
It is inside that I've died

I Was Surrounded

INSIGHT

No one wakes up and plans to be violated. No one anticipates to endure immoral, despicable, offensive crimes against them. But thank God that even when we are violated, abused, misused, mistreated, humiliated, taunted, and left uncovered, He still has the final say. God will make a way out of even the darkest situations. Some will escape in life and others will escape by death… But no matter the way out provided for us, God never leaves us. He never keeps us in a space of destitution. He gives to us who and what we need to overcome and to be victorious. When bad things happen, we should never blame God, and we should find strength to forgive. In forgiveness there is power. In our power is our ability to see that all things (good or bad) work together for our good, and for those of us who are called according to God's purpose (per the Bible).

REFLECTION

- Has anyone, known or unknown, ever violated your body?
- If so, how did you escape hating them forever?
- Who did you turn to for comfort and for help?
- Are you able to speak about this traumatic event, or is this still your secret?

PRAYER

Dear God, it is not easy to live through unimaginable events that harm us and hurt us emotionally, physically, and spiritually.

But you, God, are a God that heals us, delivers us, and sets us free. I thank you, God, for the Holy Spirit. I thank you, God, for your strength and restoration. I thank you, God, for your peace. Lord God, help the reader know that things that happen to us have consequences, and in some cases the offense is punishable by death. Comfort the reader, Lord, helping them to be free. Amen.

(Deuteronomy 22:25-27)

If only this was easy...

Her:

He loves me then leaves me
Acts like he needs me
And the next minute
it seems that he doesn't see me

His lack of dedication fills my life with procrastination
I gave up wifey benefits to him too soon
Now in the direction of marriage he won't move

He believes that I won't leave him
Does he deserve my love unconditional?
When he brings nothing to me original

But guess what, I love him anyway

Him:

I love that she allows me husband privileges
I always get hugs and kisses
She wants to be my Mrs.
But our love language is different
It causes me to be distant

I am comfortable in her life and I plan to stay

Who needs validation from a marriage license, anyway?

She already cooks and she cleans
And she makes more money than me
I'd be a fool to leave

But the truth is, I don't feel like I measure up
I love her, really, I do, but I feel stuck

The big question:

Will this man step up?
Will this woman redefine their relationship?
Or will they both quit?
Or will their loneliness become a habit
like re-stitching old fabric?
Or will they seize each moment and grab it?
How they respond determines if their love song will play long
Or will it forever be gone…
If only this was easy!

If only this was easy...

INSIGHT

If things were easy all the time, wouldn't you become bored? Perhaps. But love should never bore you. It should flow through you and hold your interest. Because love is a verb. Love moves to move people. It creates a space to release endorphins and euphoria. Love is pleasant. It is yearned for by every boy, girl, woman, and man. Love is the Great I Am. So... Why doesn't love always follow through? Let me be the first to tell you that this isn't true. Love has given us all free will. Some will take it very seriously while others choose to play the field. But be confident in knowing it is always up to you to assign your time with love appropriately.

REFLECTION

- How many times have you fallen for someone who gave you mixed signals?
- Did you allow this behavior to continue, or did you put them in the friend zone?
- Have you ever taken the chance on love and it worked out?
- Did that chance lead you to the altar?

PRAYER

Most gracious and heavenly Father, help the reader to determine the difference between how they feel and what is real. Give them, Lord, divine direction as they engage in their relationships. Loose fear from their life. Let their desire to be

unified with one soul come to pass. Let them remember to honor and glorify you in all ways and for the rest of their days. Shower them, Lord, forever with your favor. Amen.
(Psalm 143:8)

ℐezebels

They seek you to keep you under their spell.
You'll fall in love with their hips, their tits, their tips, and their smell.
They rob you of all innocence while turning down the volume on love,
and amplifying lust.

You begin to lose respect for your values, for what's real, for trust.

Jezebels will game you with their alluring smile and charm. As innocent as they may look… they inflict spiritual harm.

They will lie with you and play with you, and offer ecstasy beyond what your mind, heart, body, and soul can comprehend.

The things they do to you that now feel *so* good… once would offend.

You are so entangled in desire that your interpersonal encounters take you higher and higher.

Human touch now rots your soul with burning lust. Instead of hugs and kisses, you desire two inches more than before, or a womb deep enough to explore.

You enjoy Jezebels so much that you now seek them… and are weak for them.
Finding someone to screw because you're geeked for the touch of them.

Now sowing your wild oats is a project.
And finding participants is a process,
But you remain eager to conquer your next conquest.
Jezebels have you obsessed!

You learn that without intimacy or infatuation, your soul cannot be fed.
The thoughts of ecstasy and lust defiles your bed.

Your energy is only enough for your next rendezvous.

The question is: Are you becoming Jezebel, or is Jezebel becoming you?

Soul ties are real
So be careful whose soul you steal
For no one eats an orange and its peel
Jezebels make what is fake appear real

Now you know that it's easier than you think to be tied to the scent of lust
Laying up with people you don't trust

To come out from under this faith in God is a must

To burn away lust's scent… you must repent
Disconnect yourself from lust's insanity
Release lust's grip on your reality
It will have you thinking you have immortality

The desire of Jezebel will make every cell in your body throb
The thinking of your mind and the use of your time it robs

Jezebels are a plethora of whores who keep you coming back for more
They don't care if you are male or female
And for every Jezebel, there's a spiritual jail
Called HELL!

Jezebels

INSIGHT

It is so very easy to get caught off guard by someone who reaches beyond the surface of your existence. The type of person who draws energy from every private part of you. They ignite passion and awaken dormant cells in your body, or they take active cells and make them respond on a new level. They will have you chasing the high of their touch. You will look for them in every partner you pursue. And the cycle will begin. You will start taking from others what has been taken from you. Your mind and heart will silence, while your body experiences the highs and lows of lust. The only one who can save you from you is God. To be saved you must know him and accept his love and salvation. Don't miss out on your deliverance!

REFLECTION

- Have you met someone who made you crave their scent, their body heat, their essence?
- How did you determine if what you crave from them was/is love or lust?
- Are you able to live without daily satisfaction or sexual release?
- Do you seek others to satisfy you when that special someone becomes unavailable?

PRAYER

Heavenly Father, please allow the reader to free themselves from anyone who has created a significant bond that is meant to enthrall, deceive, and manipulate them. Father, help them see that you are the only one who can free them from the soul that ties them to immorality. I pray that the reader who is experiencing the grip of lust in their lives will fall to their knees right now in the mighty name of Jesus, repenting of their sins. And I thank you, Father, for their deliverance. For there is none like you nor will there ever be. For our sins have already been taken up on the cross and there is nothing that we cannot overcome without our faith in you. Amen.

(1 Thessalonians 4:3-5)

Let Freedom Ring

I am uneasy and insecure about the mystery that lies behind door #1.
Hopefully, whoever is behind this door will hold my freedom papers.
I want to be free!

My back aches and my feet are sore; my sweat rains out from every pore.
I am one tired ole soul. Can't take no more royal beatings and mistreatings...
I needs me some peace on dis here old earth.
Lord knows I got sold cheaper than what I'm really worth.

They try to mentally break me down, wound me from the inside first.
They say things like monkey girl, ugly, dogface, and nigga bitch...

These words don't faze me because I know in God's kingdom,
I'm considered among the rich.

After raping me and degrading me,
They repeatedly slash my skin.
After all the torment is over,
My spirit feels completely broken.

I catch my reflection from a fragment of glass left from a broken bottle.
All the brutal comments that were told to me… fade away.
My nappy hair, saddened eyes, jelly roll, and ham hock thighs,
Enhance my voluptuous figure…
And I would still love myself if I were a couple pounds bigger.

America has me trapped!
I don't want to be here any longer.
But how will I know if Africa feels like my home?
Since I was sold as an infant and now I'm fully grown.

The other slave women were kind enough to teach me about my Savior.
They told me how to act, and about the consequences of my behavior.
Even taught me to read and write…
I'd secretly practice writing to get my signature tight.

I want my handwriting perfect on my freedom papers.
I need to be freed from the misses, masters, and racists.

My heart and hopes had been broken so many times before.

Now I'm saved and wiser.
My mental and physical strength has gotten stronger.
Those negative comments and tortures can break my spirit no
longer.

They tease with my right of freedom.
For they know how much I need them.
But one day I'll enjoy the mystery behind door #1.
For now, I pray that freedom will ring until the falling sun.

Let Freedom Ring

INSIGHT

We take our freedoms for granted. We do not realize all who paved the way and endured torturous, horrific, and unforgiving conditions, so that we can walk around coexisting with other races and cultures without immediate fear of our lives. Ancestors have had their hearts beat to humiliation, segregation, and degradation. But there is revelation in God's word. You won't know this unless you read for yourself.

REFLECTION

- Can you imagine yourself being enslaved?
- Would you be able to endure harsh conditions?
- How have you paid tribute to your ancestors?

PRAYER

Heavenly Father, please encourage the reader to remember their roots and the plight of their ancestors. Give them the strength to weather their current situations. Order their steps, Lord, and follow them all the days of their life. Amen. (Galatians 5:1)

Liar Liar

Liar! Liar! Pants on fire
Can't look at you with admiring eyes
All your lies
I despise

You almost took away my identity
Robbed me of my inner self
Instead of pretending to love me
You should have left

One plus one
Made a creation
Three minus one
Leaves devastation

The tragedy of love
Is love not returned
The gift of love
Is lessons learned

Liar Liar

INSIGHT

Have you ever loved someone with all your heart? Investing your time, attention, and hopes in a future with them? Thinking that they wanted the same things, but finding out in time that everything they told you about loving you was lies? Even after creating life with them, they still found no value in maintaining a level of accountability, stability, or respect for you or for themselves. Their lies created brokenness in their offspring, and brokenness inside of you, too. But thank God that He mends our broken hearts. He fills us with joy. He anoints us with valor. He reminds us that His love never fails. I thank God for His presence and for His deliverance.

REFLECTION

- Have someone's lies completely turned your life upside down?
- Did their lies cause you to be bitter, or did you forgive them?
- Were you able to pick up the pieces and move on, or are you still holding on?

PRAYER

Most gracious and heavenly Father, it is very painful when we are fooled. It is humiliating and makes us question our judge of character. God, free the reader from humiliation. Free them from heartache and shame. Help them, Lord, come to you in prayer for everything. Help them be still and learn to wait on you. Help them to rely on their intuition. Help them call out to the Holy Spirit for guidance. Reassure them, God, that whatever is taken away from them can be restored by faith. Help them rely on your love and on your joy. Give them strength to move on. Amen. (Proverbs 26:24-25)

Lied

Tried to stop loving you, but can't
The hurt and pain of betrayal inflicted
upon my soul… shattered my being

But left for me a story to tell
No one knows how deep a love can brew
Until love happens to you

A love so satisfying, and gratifying, and undenying
A love so full of lust, full of rage, and full of pain
Two lovers seeing at a different point of view
But love so powerful between the two

Passion filled
Then passion slips away
Your center pulsates
The beat of your heart flutters

The stiffening of his member makes you smile
The feel... The feel is amazing
A child is born from a day fuck
That chills you...
But to him it meant nothing

A rendezvous with a moonlit sky
Enhances the mood and creates a flow
Her false quivers and afterglow
Led him to believe... that he laid his pipe
Like the ding-a-ling king
To him it was unforgettable
To her it meant nothing

Disappointment dances around the air
Two people with love and respect
Have now burned out and can no longer connect
Who said love was simple?

Do you believe in each one... reach one... teach one?
Can you reach me to teach me and draw from my energy?

Can you let the past bury itself?

Who said love was simple?

Can it be like riding a bike
In love by day and lovers by night
Do you desire to get things right?
Put up a fight
Create a union tight

Forgiveness is big in settling the score
Let's just keep it real and hard to the core
Taking time to explore
The rarity of love through the rain
the sunshine and the pain

Love gives us something to live for
But whoever said that love was simple, lied

Let's Inspire Each other Daily

Lied

INSIGHT

Love is supposed to be easy. Love is an action. It moves, it flows, it showers, it covers, it forgives, it thanks, it cares about you. Love satisfies you even when you are sad. Love doesn't hold secrets or grudges against you. Love will provide you peace on a battlefield. Love endures all things and hopes all things. Love never fails. Love is yearned for all over the world, and is the most desired feeling. Love heals. Love helps. Love restores. Love gives. Love is honest. It is faithful. It is true. It is the one word used over and over again… but how often is this word misused? How often does someone say they love you and it feels like a lie?

There is good news! God is a God that never lies, and his love for us is forever.

REFLECTION

- Have you ever said I love you and not meant it?
- If so, did you do this to get something you wanted from someone you had no intentions of loving?
- How did it make you feel when you realized that someone you loved no longer loved you?

PRAYER

Heavenly Father, maker of heaven and earth. The one who knows what is, what was, and what is to come. Thank you for loving us through difficult times. Thank you for your grace and mercy. Thank you for sacrificing your only begotten son for us. Thank you for saving us from the traps of the enemy. Father, help the reader know that they can never love even themselves without knowing your love for them first. Without realizing that you are love, and you love without measure. Lord, uncover our blind spots, so that we can see and feel the love that lives within us. Amen.

(1 Corinthians 13:4-7)

No More Hate

You hate me on the mere fact that I do not look like you
You hate me because you were taught that I am ugly and unclean
You hate me because the spirit inside of you is loyal to sin and mean

You hate me because, unlike you, I love God and all His goodness
You hate me because I don't apologize for being God's witness

But you fail to see that we all bleed red
You fail to see that if you were hungry
I'd make sure you were fed
You fail to see that our money spends the same
You fail to see that we both get wet when it rains

While you are busy hating me
I am busy loving you in spite of

While you are busy hating me
I am praying for your deliverance

While you are busy hating me
I am celebrating my victories

Hate is an emotion that causes people to be heavily attached
to sin
It wrongfully accuses and consciously abuses people different
than them

Hate is a replica of disease
It finds its host, settles in
and won't let them breathe

It jades their common sense and compassion
It smothers their dreams, making them feel like a has-been

The idea that someone can hate by color, race, gender, or creed
is perplexing

To conquer hate, you would have to be more than an answer
to a lesson
You would have to become a blessing

About Love:

Love moves forward even in water that is still
It's the hope that in time all things are revealed

So instead of hating me:

Help me
Encourage me
Acknowledge me
Learn about me

Because love could never hate you

No More Hate

INSIGHT

Living day in and day out filled with hate must be exhausting. Hurt people enjoy the drama of watching you lose your mind. Hate will cause you to be buried neck deep in confusion. It makes the vision of the hater askew. Hate plots, plans, and promotes misery. The good news is the love of God will free you from hate. The love of God will make hate vanish from within. The love of God will sustain you forever (through the end of time).

REFLECTION

- Have you or someone you know ever been discriminated against or rejected because of what you/they look like?
- If so, did you report it, or did you face it alone?
- What helped you to move on?
- Are you willing to bring awareness to the atrocities of hate in love and in peace?

PRAYER

Father God, it is in the mighty name of Jesus that I ask you to lift and remove the strongholds of hate from the reader. If they are harboring any ill will or unforgiveness in their hearts, Lord, that is causing their love to be further and further away from you, please break the stronghold and extend to them new grace and new mercy. Help them to recover from the remnants of the pain that hate has caused, and restore their faith in you as they begin to operate in agape love. Amen.

(1 John 2:9-11)

No Shame

You branded me an outsider before you got to know me
Thought I heard you calling me dirty
Straight up disrespecting my name
In my face you lie to me

Do you not have any shame?

You try to convince me that the riches on your back
Are far more impressive than the sincerity of the heart
But I'm not impressed
Because I do not worship material things
I'd rather have peace of mind than the false shine from bling

The jealousies that lie within you
Keep your days sad with envy
I don't want a contrite heart
With the thoughts of "that's mine" and "give me"

You whisper softly in my ear for me to jump from bed to bed
The desires of the flesh will eventually end you dead
And you invite me to every party... though I always decline
It's bad enough I love the pig... but I refuse to drink your wine

I am not moved by quick pleasures or temporary delight
Ya see, I only walk with Jesus
For He is the truth, the way, and the life
And in my Father's house are many mansions
And I know one has my name

If you repent and believe in the Lord
You too can have the same
And begin living your life
Completely free of shame

No Shame

INSIGHT

In our lives, we will connect with people who are not like-minded with us. People who do not care about consequences, because the sins they enjoy pleasure them greater than the outcome. The question is, will you pretend to live like them, speak like them, enjoy sin like them? Or will you unapologetically share the salvation of Jesus Christ with them? Will you declare Jesus as your Lord and Savior in front of them? Will you let them know about eternal life and the kingdom of heaven? Will you have no shame for Jesus?

REFLECTION

- Is there anyone in your life who lives their life loosely?
- Have you introduced them to God's love?
- Have you offered to pray with them?
- Or is that someone you?

PRAYER

Father God, help the reader who struggles with the pleasures of the world humble themselves, giving you all glory, honor, and praise. Lord, bless them and give to them wisdom to depart from their old ways and activities. Give them the desire to witness in your name and share your goodness and salvation in the land of the living. Let them sing, dance, and rejoice in your name without fear or concern. Let them live out the rest of their days for you and shameless. Amen.
(1 Peter 3:14-19)

Out of Darkness

Celebrating with tears or fears throughout the years
All I see is myself all alone
Taking trips to the park, or brisk walks of any season
I reason to myself… I'm still alone

Happy holidays or Sunday's praise
I pinch myself… I'm all alone

Locked in a dark room
Absolutely no sunlight coming through
I touch myself… Still I'm alone

As I lie down to sleep
My eyes open
But my mind is closed
I hear a voice and get no feeling in my toes
A still calm runs through my veins

My hands begin to sweat
My heart... quickens in pace
I feel a presence
But I see no face

Tiny beams of light bounce off my walls
The sweat of my brow... beads then crawls
No longer alone and feeling my breath decrease
All bodily fluids are brought up or released

No more locked doors, for I am alone no more
I see a world for me to conquer and explore
Allowing myself to slip out of that state of mind was the best thing for me
Learning that my Savior helped the negative to flee
Opting to live life's every moment
Never giving in to my opponent
Each night I pray, "Thank you, Lord, for visiting my home"

For never again am I ALONE

Out of Darkness

INSIGHT

Have you ever been in a crowded room and you still did not feel present or connected to its people or the event? Have you ever spent hours crying at night because you felt there was no one in the world who could relate to your fear, your sadness, your disappointment, your rejection, your pain? Have you ever tried telling someone your story, but they were only focused on themselves? Loneliness carries with it disconnection. The enemy wants you to be disconnected from God and all of His promises. The Word of God tells us that our friends may not always be there. That our parents may not always be there. But there is a friend who will stick closer to us than a brother (Proverbs 18:24) and his name is Jesus. Jesus does not leave us or disown us. He is there in the morning and in the midnight hour. Wherever we go, He is also. You have to know this and believe this with your whole heart, and the shackles meant to separate and destroy your faith will be broken.

REFLECTION

- Have you ever felt separated from the love of God?
- How did you reconnect to His love and to His grace?
- Are you free from the spell of loneliness?
- Are you prepared to reject loneliness when it tries to hold you in bondage?

PRAYER

Father God, in the mighty and matchless name of Jesus, I pray that the reader finds comfort in knowing that you are with them 24/7, every day of the week. That even in their times of loneliness... you, Lord God, are there. Lord God, I pray that nothing separates the reader from your love. And I pray that the shackles of loneliness be broken and forever removed from their lives. Amen.

(James 4:8)

Plans for Me

I have amazing parents (Brenda & Lewis Thompson) and the bestest sister (LaTonya Hickman)! I have amazing church friends, and awesome best friends (Christine Andrews and Donnita Fowler). I have awesome sister friends (Regina Ball, Christy Cooper, Lonnie Evans, Sherry Glover, Heidi Obando, Mary Olapidupido, and Bridgette Spencer) and the most caring children (Larenai & John Swann) and nephews (Jaron & Christopher Hickman), as well as an amazing brother-in-love (Jaron Hickman I), cousins, uncles, aunties, godchildren, and a granddad like no other. I have the love of God in my life, which keeps me from growing weary…

With all the love from people in my life, nothing feels scary.

I am *so* blessed…!

Blessed that my parents pray for me, asking God to have His way.

Blessed that Donnita prays with me and for me at any time of the night or day.

Blessed that my sister prays for me and shows me unconditional love.

Blessed that OJ and William Hawkins are more to me than a cuz.

Blessed that my children accepted Christ early in their lives.

Blessed that my many talks with my granddad help me to see past the devil's lies.

Thank you, God, for I know you have plans for me!

Plans for me to speak to millions of men and women.

Plans to share with them your love and your brilliance.

Plans to make the words in my heart change many lives.

Plans to make single women see themselves as wives.

Plans that will manifest and, in return, all the glory you will get.

Thank you, Lord, for believing in me, for I have no plans to quit!

Plans for Me

INSIGHT

We all make plans to succeed. Plans to prosper. Plans to grow. Plans to excel. If our plans do not align with God's plans for us, or His will, the road to success will include pitfalls, dead ends, wrong turns, delays, and much more. You cannot plan to make it without God. God will move obstacles and road-blocks from your path. He will get you to the right people, and make sure that these people are in position to move you forward or closer to your dreams/goals. It is important to trust God. It is important to thank Him. And it is important to give Him praise. For God will propel you to your destiny. And remember that God does not walk ahead or behind us. God walks with us.

REFLECTION

- What dream do you have that you would like to come into fruition?
- Are you working towards making your dream come true?
- Have you written down your goals and aspirations or created a vision board to help keep you on track?
- Have you asked Jesus to order your steps and show you His way?

PRAYER

Lord God, we are lost without you. We cannot win without you. You have given us <u>B</u>asic <u>I</u>nstructions <u>B</u>efore <u>L</u>eaving <u>E</u>arth. Let the reader never give up on their dreams. Let them always consult with you. Let them take the steps necessary to fulfill their dreams. Remind them, Lord, that when they move, you will move also. And that anything that is idle is inactive. Lord, activate their faith and reestablish them in your will. Amen. (Jeremiah 29:11)

Pray

When tired, afraid, alone, dismayed…
Pray!
When sad, rejected, at loss for words, disrespected…
Pray!
When hopeless, confused, mistreated, abused…
Pray!
For the word of God says: 1st Thessalonians 5:17
Pray without ceasing.
When we pray, we are talking to our Father who art in heaven.
When we pray, we are sharing our concern and announcing our reverence.
We are allowing the Lord thy God access and believing in the process.
If God did it for Abraham, Isaac, and Jacob, will He not do it for you?
Will He not guide and provide for you?
Will He not shield and protect you, too?

YOU ARE NOT YOUR CIRCUMSTANCE!

The things you go through will strengthen you, stretch you, grow you, and restore you...

and in God's time show you who is and who is not for you.

Tragedy. Loss. Suffering.

Will come.

It seems as if a storm is always near.

But learn to activate your faith to cancel out your fear.

Ya see, fear is sent as it is meant.

The enemy plants a seed of doubt in hopes that it will sprout.

Learn to rejoice, give thanks, and praise.

The Lord God promises us that troubles won't last always.

John 3:16

For God so loved the world, that he gave his only begotten son, that whosoever believeth in him shall not perish, but will have everlasting life.

In this lifetime there will NEVER be a greater sacrifice.

So, when you are faced with challenges, problems, and doubts...

When the world seems so dark and there's no way out...

STOP trying to do things your way...

and PRAY!

Pray

INSIGHT

To overcome obstacles and distractions in your life, it begins with you having a conversation with God. You must pray (Praise. Repent. Ask. Yield)! Prayer is us talking to God, and reading God's Word is God talking to us.

The devil loves confusion and chaos. He loves when we make our problems bigger than our God. He loves visiting us at our weakest moments. To shut the devil out, you must start with Prayer. You must have a conversation with God in Jesus' name. And just like us, God does not like one-sided relationships. Start by acknowledging God and all His goodness. Give him His due reverence. Tell Him how awesome He is. Profess what you have done, or what you are doing, that you know is not pleasing to Him. Then repent. Ask God to forgive you (and never do it again—which is easier said than done, but you must try wholeheartedly), and yield to His will and to His way, never doubting His sacrifice, love, or intentions.

REFLECTION

- What keeps you up at night that you are unwilling to talk about?
- Have you made prayer in your life a priority?
- Do you make time in your life to mature your relationship with God?

PRAYER

Heavenly Father, the one who is loved and adored. The one who loves us without judgement or condition. The one who reigns in our lives forever. You are an awesome God! A mighty, mighty good God. I ask that the reader is blessed in every area of their life, Lord. I pray in Jesus' name that the reader confesses to you what is bothering them. I pray that the reader surrenders all to you. I pray that they begin talking to you more. I pray that when they read your Word and listen to you, that every stronghold in their life be broken. Lord, I thank you right now in the matchless name of Jesus, believing it is so, as it is written. Amen.

(Jeremiah 29: 12-13)

Released

I am no longer authorized to hear what you must say
Life with you has been one big pause or delay
But there is a real peace about being released
No more teary eyes or compromise
No more watching or waiting and selling me dreams
No more getting stuck in humdrum activities and routines
The sin you offered soothed my scars and gave me freedom to think
That what I was doing and where I was headed was quite unique
Years 1-3 was me discovering me
Years 3-5 was me figuring why you cheated and lied, yet I stayed by your side
Years 6, 7, 8 I didn't understand why there was no wedding date
Years 9-12 God met me where I was and showed me His love
Years 13-15 was flatlined… Dead inside
Needed REVIVAL
I started to pray and attend church,

Steadily talking to God, but I started listening to Him too
I tried to share this good news with you
But you were jaded from your past
and your past has shaped you and your future
Your past experienced you!
Your past created the demons in which you allow to live
and the things that a relationship needs, you are unable to give
Oh, how I tried to love you, to love us, to love me
Without God at the forefront of both our lives, the love that we created could never be
I began to repent, I began to cry out and pray, I began to see who was the truth, the life, and the way
There was a time that access was granted to you and you took it all for granted
Thinking that I was going to be around forever
God's plans, though we may not understand them, changed that
In fact, God is the only one who can offer forever and mean it
In rediscovering God, my addiction to you became less and less
The Holy Spirit began allowing me to experience firsthand words like:
JOY, LOVE, PEACE, HAPPINESS, BLESSED
Thank you for loving me from uno to quince... for none of this time I regret
But being divinely released from you helps me look forward to my best years yet.
~~P.S. Nothing grows without God and change~~

Released

INSIGHT

The longer you allow the wrong attachment in your life, the longer it will take for your life to move forward. And what you are around, in time, you will eventually become. If you are around people who are always afraid… before you know it, everything will make you apprehensive. If you are around people who accept mediocrity and do not set goals… in time, procrastination will become a habit of yours. The good news is you do not have to stay around people who are not right for you. For if you do, you will not change them, but they will inevitably change you. And this is not just a yin-yang thing, or a weird folklore—this is Word.

REFLECTION

- Do you give people a thousand chances to show you that their behavior towards you will get better?
- Do you associate with like-minded people?
- If not, have you noticed a change in your own behavior and expectations?

PRAYER

Dear Lord, the one who sits high and looks low… please release the reader from people who show them inconsistent behavior. From people who take their kindness for weakness. From people who pretend to like them only to use them. Release them, Lord, from anything or anyone who is not approved by you. Give them the will to move forward in their life even if it is alone, and let them never be caught up in other people's false promises again. Amen.
(1 Corinthians 15:33)

Shift

Somewhere along the line, roles reversed and became the new norm.

Shift!

Men got manicures and women fixed cars.

Shift!

Education and who brought home the bacon changed.

Shift!

Family life and boundaries fade.

Shift!

Loyalty and commitment, do they exist?

Shift!

Is domestic violence worth that risk?

Shift!

Each generation says their times were the good ole days.

Shift!

If this were true, would new generations overwhelmingly end up in graves?

Shift!

Each day will always bring about shift... The question is, will you be life's burden or gift?

Think about it.

Shift

INSIGHT

Have you ever wondered why people or things change, even though there are pre-set rules or requirements in place to avoid disorder, misunderstandings, or unreasonable compromise? Often, it's not financial status, environment, or values that need to change… It is the changing of the mindset. And all change is not bad. It's only bad if it is allowed to manifest hate, disrespect, mean-spiritedness, selfishness, bitterness, unfriendliness, abusiveness, or elusiveness in your spirit. The goal is to change with the times without letting the times change you. If change scares you, the Word tells us that God is the same, yesterday, today, and forever (Hebrews 13:8). He is the one constant you just can depend on to remain the same at all times. God will always be loving, accepting, and available. So before conforming to role reversals, or outdated traditions, or the world… Remember to seek God's promises. For his promises have stood the test of time again, and again, and again, and no one will ever be able to change this.

REFLECTION

- Have you kept up with traditions that were passed down through your family?
- Are you able to stay true to your character in the midst of chaos?
- How do you feel when the familiar becomes unfamiliar?

PRAYER

Lord God, thank you for being the one true constant in the reader's life. Thank you for being there in every challenge, change, and conformity that has presented itself to them. Shift their atmosphere when needed to keep them in a good head-space. And let every new thing in their life birth a blessing for them and what they are attached to. Amen.

(James 1:17)

Sleep Child Sleep

Young, Black, Beautiful
14 years to the grave
Her environment had her enslaved

She touched too much
She smiled too much
Loved a crowd too much

The things they thought she knew
She actually had no clue
But who would figure
That the killer that pulled the trigger
Owned her daddy's name
She was way too young to know
She was getting caught up in the game

Now rainbows and angels encircle her
The world she once knew will no longer hurt her

Sleep, child, sleep
For heaven is upon you
Sleep, child,sleep
We'll forever miss your smile
Sleep in peace
Our Young, Black, Beautiful child

Sleep Child Sleep

INSIGHT

It is important to be aware of the places you go and the company you choose to keep. Even members of your family can be wolves dressed as sheep. Give yourself time to see people for who they are to avoid mishaps, misjudgments, and miscommunication. No one will ever love you like the Lord. Are you strong enough to fight even those closest to you with your sword (the Bible)? It is important to always be spiritually woke to avoid dying prematurely.

REFLECTION

- What activities do you participate in that make you feel guilty?
- Do you trust others easily without verifying facts about them or their spirit?
- Do you easily give in to peer pressure?

PRAYER

Father God, in the mighty name of Jesus, I am calling out to you to give the reader spiritual sight so that they can clearly see when danger is in their mist. Lord, bring forth wisdom and discernment like a strong, raging wind to wake up the reader and give them strength to be free from the traps of their environment. Let nothing and no one lead them astray. And assign those closest to them as their protectors to help keep them away from negative influences and away from those who plan to damage them and inflict harm to them. Amen.
(Psalm 121:8)

The Man I Desire

I want to live out the rest of my days

with a man who also lives within the will of God.

A man who has mutual respect for me.

Someone who puts our relationship first and is able to provide.

Someone who can make me laugh and who is generous with their time and money.

Someone who is not afraid to be emotionally naked around me.

A man who shares my vision.

A man who loves me enough to listen.

A man who enjoys separate hobbies but still we grow together.

A man who is patient with me, and speaks kind words, shows appreciation and compassion.

A man who can disagree and disagree without drama.

A man who doesn't lie to me, not even about small things.

Someone who is trustworthy, full of integrity, and exhibits honesty.

A man who my closest relatives and friends see in him the same things I see.

A man who sees my value and chooses for us marriage.

A man who doesn't get easily discouraged.

God, send me a man who honors you in spirit and in truth.

Send me a Boaz like you sent to Ruth.

The Man I Desire

INSIGHT

It's a natural desire to want unity. To want affection. To want commitment and dedication. These are things that should come easy. But for some, these things do not come easy at all. Because God makes each of us unalike in many ways. Trying to spiritually connect with someone who is on the same page as you, or shares your goals, and respects your dreams, is like sifting through tiny grains of sand to find a metal ring. It is not impossible, but it takes time to happen.

REFLECTION

- While you wait for your desires to manifest, what are you doing in your spare time?
- Do you agree that opposites attract, or is your philosophy "birds of a feather will flock together"?
- In social gatherings, does being single make you feel uncomfortable?

PRAYER

Father God, assure the reader there is still power and purpose in their singleness. Teach them that being a good steward, a faithful disciple, and a wonderful witness in your name will give them the gifts they need to sustain longevity in the union with their spouse who is yet to come. Amen.
(Proverbs 18:22)

The Son of a Preacher Man

Nan-Nanny-Nan-Na, suck your momma's tittie ball
Then the bell sounds and ends it all
Tiny beings race to form a line
All saddened because recess is over
There are always a few who break the rules
Like Big Bad Willie and his goons
They sneak off to smoke, joke, and goof around
One day Big Bad Willie left the playground
And could not be found
Of course, the kids did not care
They felt free when Willie wasn't there

It's a shame because Wee Little Willie was the son
of a preacher man... and Little Willie ran into

his father's deacon friend
He approached the young child with a grin
But Big Bad Willie wasn't afraid... after all
this was a familiar face
That same face took the lad to an unfamiliar place
and forever changed his life
He strategically placed duct tape on his mouth
Handcuffed his hands and legs to the bed poles
His lust was so thick and mental so sick
He kissed up and down the boy's back
and fingered his crack

Tears just flowed and time stood still
The only thing Willie thought of was when will
Jesus let this nightmare stop

Then it happened
The unforgettable and unforgiveable
The deacon entered young Willie
His strokes were long and strong
A young spirit wronged
The blood, the tears, the bruises
How could anyone do this?

How could this happen to the son of a preacher man

Willie's young body began to limp
As he slipped in and out of unconsciousness
The boy who once tormented a whole school
Now was some else's whore

The man slapped him
"Wake up"
The man slapped him again
"Wake up, you weak fuck"
But Willie had left his body
The same way he had left the school
He was a child trying to escape a complex life
Now he lies still until the cops find his remains

The deacon was a coward
Who loved to inflict pain
But Willie's life wasn't in vain
You see, although Little Willie had been a coward too
And could not face a day without tormenting someone's child
He also was a public speaker
He punked every child in the crowd
Because he was trapped in a world of perfection to make his
father proud

Willie's father taught him several things, but not when to be
alarmed
The deacon was a full-on demon that raped, hurt, and harmed.

Life may be a three-sixty
But nothing this awful should ever come around
So be careful what you do, pay attention to others' behavior
And don't straddle the line between the devil and your Savior

Now the child who lived a double life
Perfect on Sunday and Hell Raiser on Monday
Can never pursue his dreams

Did I mention that Willie could sing

The deacon was caught and brought to justice
An inmate did the same thing he did to Willie to him
He thought his hell was on earth
Until his death served him a spot in eternal heat

The preacher man prayed
"Father, help your children, for they know not what they do"
Deacon's soul floated around
For he knew what he had done
And if he hadn't been stopped
The next child could've been your son

The Son of a Preacher Man

INSIGHT

If what goes around comes around, why do people still choose to lie, cheat, steal, misbehave, abuse, hurt one another, and murder? It is important to treat others the way you want to be treated, because karma does not care about age, nationality, or social status. What we do to others will not only affect the victims, but it will affect your bloodline. A good tree will bear good fruit, and a bad tree will bear the opposite. A man or woman of good character will do what is right in God's sight, whether they have an audience or not.

REFLECTION

- Have you ever been bullied or mistreated?
- If so, what did you do to come out of that situation alive?
- Who do you need to forgive to remove the bitterness of karma from your life?

PRAYER

Most gracious and heavenly Father, evildoers are all around. They seek to devour and have no remorse. But you, Lord God, are a just God, and you take mighty good care of those who have faith and believe in you. I am asking you, Lord, to heal the reader of any trauma that has placed a seed of revenge on the inside of them. Lord God, for the battle is not ours—it is yours. And we trust this as it is written. Amen.
(Galatians 6:7)

Too Quick to Trust

People treasure different things.
Some people treasure gifts,
Some people treasure cards or gold,
Some people treasure mysteries untold.

But no one knows how good a treasure can be…
Until someone takes it for free.

Life gives people all sorts of stop signs, green lights, twists and
turns, and roads that end…
But does life give us people whom we can call a true friend?

What is a true friend, anyway?
Is it someone who calls to brighten your day?
Or is a friend someone who listens from the heart…
Someone who is levelheaded, caring, and smart?

No one knows exactly how true a friend can be...
Until something happens to break up their history.

There is a truth for people of all ages to hear... It happened to a young girl just this year.

Off to school on a Tuesday this young girl went, not knowing that things were going to happen to her in such an event.

After school, the young girl was with her best friend,
And something told her to go her own way.

Without a good reason, in her best friend's company she decided to stay.

The girl went with her best friend to see her new place,
The girl never expected to see her best friend's boyfriend's face.

Time and time went by as they all chitted and chatted
As the boyfriend got ready to leave
The girl asked him for a ride, never thinking that this man was going to literally change her forever inside.

She had no doubts as she got into his car.
This is when the story gets a little bizarre.

"Straight to the train station," he was told.
Never making it to the train station, the intentions of this man's desires started to unfold.

They made a stop to his home, he asked her to stay.
Not knowing that his lust for her was coming her way,

Too quick to trust him, though her intuition told her to run.
The devastation of this experience would burn hotter than the
sun.

Ya see, she saw him as her friend,
But he saw himself as her man.
The things he asked shocked her ears,
But this girl wasn't frightened...
Because she had known him for some time,
And had known her best friend for years.

The girl made it clear that she would NEVER go his way,
So he calmed down and made her feel comfortable to stay.
The whole plan was to put his clothes in to wash, and then
leave.

But she was easy to deceive and was quite naïve.

The clothes were upstairs. "Can you help me separate them?"
he said.

He took her kindness for weakness and got her in his bed.

The poor girl was totally misled.

Of course, she told him "NO!"
And even got him to quit,
She thought she got him to change his mind,
But it never changed one bit.

He preyed on her body as if it were a piece of meat.
He acted like a wolf in heat.

He was heartless and strong…
But the girl still put up a fight,
Until she was shocked…
That he broke into her treasure of delight.

She questioned if what happened to her was meant,
She thought it had to be a part of her Master's plan.
Her heart disagreed, as she failed to understand.

People are attracted to different things,
It could be the sound of a person's voice.
It could be personality or shape…
But NO means NO!
And something sexually done against one's will
Is RAPE!

This was one Tuesday the young girl wanted to forget.
She lost her best friend.
She lost trust and her treasure.
She lost true sense to the meaning of pleasure.

Too Quick to Trust!

INSIGHT

We all have friends we think have our best interests at heart. Have you ever had a friend let you down? A friend whose significant other used you to get back at them? A friend who you wanted to make happy and, in turn, it compromised your peace, your trust, and your friendship? A friend who passed you along to their wolf? A wolf that made you experience one of your darkest days.

God allows us to rest in his bosom as we grieve and heal. He offers us comfort and unconditional love, even when we ignore His warnings. It is imperative that you trust in the Lord and never be too quick to trust in man.

REFLECTION

- Has someone taken something precious from you?
- What did you do to recover and heal?
- Did your experience amplify your discernment?

PRAYER

Heavenly Father, the one who sits high and looks low, please deliver the reader who is still reliving trauma in their lives. Free them, Lord, from any painful memories. Show them friendship through your peace and your love. Cover them with a shield of protection. Deliver them from the traumas of evil. Amen. (Roman 2:6-11)

Uncertain

Around in circles
Back in time
No end to the past
Is my rhythmic rhyme

My heart beats to loneliness
Your absence has me changed
The blindness of assumption
Has extended the length of my days

I AM PITIFUL
All the hopes of a future
Are only fantasies
Finally realized they just didn't love me

So many challenges and hidden misconceptions
I allowed my blessings to become lessons

Because doubt weakened my strength
I thought every nice deed was heaven sent

But still my mind has created a perfect past
A past for a future built to last
And, in my life's forecast is rain... rain... rain...
And the uncertainties certainly have me drained

Because they say God always takes care of fools and babies
And my foolishness has me crazy
And this depression has me lazy
Somebody... Please save me!

Uncertain

INSIGHT

"Uncertain: (adj.) Not able to be relied on; not known or definite"

Throughout the course of time, life will present uncertainty at one time in our lives or another. How you respond to it is key. Allowing what has yet to happen to destroy your peace is a surefire way to have sleepless nights, anxieties, and depression. Let God carry all your burdens because he cares for you. God will never leave you or forsake you. So even when you feel alone, God is still there. Allow yourself to feel his presence, otherwise the enemy will use your loneliness as a weapon against you.

REFLECTION

- Do you fear what you have no control over?
- Are you the person who looks at the previews before watching the show?
- Are you a person who always has to be in the know?

PRAYER

Father God, in the mighty name of Jesus, please deliver the reader from sleepless nights, night terrors, sadness, and fear. Let your Holy Ghost Power rise up on the inside of them to help them process their uneasiness. I rebuke any emotional or spiritual attack, Lord, in your name, to preserve the mental health of your people. Amen.
(Psalm 23:4)

Unfound Beauty

Clean cut
Tight Butt
Walks hand in hand

Dreams of boats, waterfalls, and platinum rings

Always hoping for these things

A partner's shoulder on which to lean

Time to wake up from this dream

Black, Ugly, with Nappy hair
The world looks for the outer
Laughing endlessly without care

Scared at night
Nervous by day
Hate yourself!
Hate yourself to be on display
Just living life meaningless
Takes all your strength to get through the day
To our Father in heaven you look up and say…
Help, Lord!
Why me?
I'm pretty inside.
Why can't they see?

 *Unfound Beauty*

INSIGHT

It takes a great deal of confidence to maneuver about in everyday life showing people who you are. How people see you can add or subtract from your self-esteem when you depend on compliments to help define you. Beauty is in all of us. We all have something nobody else has that makes us special. Something that is unique to the fiber of our DNA. Whether it is your smile, your swag, your posture, the color of your eyes, your personality, or the light you carry within… it is noticed only if you share it with confidence. Never be afraid of showing others what makes you special. We all have different features, but just like in a movie, they only come alive when we are not scared to be in the spotlight.

REFLECTION

- What is your favorite characteristic about yourself?
- Do you often look at yourself and see how beautiful and uniquely made you are?
- Is your self-esteem tied to other people's opinions about you?
- In what ways do you build your self-esteem?

PRAYER

Lord God, help the reader see just how beautiful they are. Let them walk around, not because of their confidence in themselves, but because of their confidence in you. When they begin to be free from other people's opinions about themselves, and focus on your opinion about them instead, they will walk tall, smile more, create more, give more, and be the light you have intended for them to be. Lord God, thank you for making us all beautiful and wonderfully made in your image. Amen. (Psalm 139:13-14)

Use ME

Dear Lord,

My passion ignites me, and excites me, and sparks my imagination.

When I see a blank piece of paper, I write.

When I see a blank screen, I type.

When I hear a dope beat, I rhyme.

When I feel joy, I'm crying.

When I see a broken heart, I pray!

When I see the sick... these hands I lay.

I go to spiritual war for all I reach.

I use my sword as a tool to teach.

Some would say I preach!

Yet I write and sing, and I reach and I teach and I proclaim and explain and cause legions to flee... even with all this I don't know what my calling will be.

I want to name it and use it and never ever lose it.

I want to know... will my passion grow?

Will my sacrifice show?

Dear Lord, use me as you see fit.

I'm ready.

Use ME

INSIGHT

Gifts and talents are placed on the inside of you in advance for the sole purpose to edify and exalt the Lord, to help build up His kingdom, and to witness in His name. But one of the most asked questions is: What is my purpose? To know what your purpose is, you must know what spiritual gifts or talents you have. And knowing what your spiritual gifts and talents are will help you answer that question.

REFLECTION

- Do your gifts and talents align with the will of God?
- Do you make room for your gifts and talents to grow?
- Have you shared your gifts and talents with others, or are you keeping them to yourself?

PRAYER

Most gracious and merciful Father, thank you for giving the reader specific talents and gifts to aid in building up your Kingdom. Show them, Lord, what you want from them. Show them what is necessary to bring others to you in Jesus' name. Let them not take the ability to communicate, create, listen, or give for granted. And let the use of their senses be heightened as they learn, grow, and prosper, while being a blessing to others. Amen.

(Ephesians 2:10)

Want to Be Heard

I want to feel respected
I want to feel that my voice is heard and that my opinions matter
I want to feel that I add value
I want to feel that my performance is trusted

Hear me, Oh Lord, and Free me!
Help my voice sound off like the energy left behind by an atomic bomb
Or play louder than their favorite song
Or echo bigger than a cymbal's gong

What must be done for my opinions to manifest
For them to see me at my best
And turn those no's into a yes

Hear me, Oh Lord, and Free me!

When will they finally see me?

Want to be Heard

INSIGHT

We carry power in our voice. The softer we speak, the more we are ignored. People respond to loud confidence. Right or wrong, the loudest in the room usually gets the most attention. But know that God sees and hears everything. He will hear your prayers and connect you to people, places, and things that will propel you. He may even use the voice of another for you to be heard as He did with Moses. Even while these things may be true, never be afraid to speak up. Usually when you do, you will find that other people are just as afraid.

REFLECTION

- Can you recall a time that you were unable to articulate your idea, concern, or interpretation because someone started speaking up and over you?
- How did that make you feel?
- How did you advocate for yourself?

PRAYER

Heavenly Father, please hear the heart of the reader. Let their desires manifest, and give them the tools to use and courage to speak up. Let them never again sit on an idea that is meant to be heard due to their low volume or low frequency. Let all things connected to you, Lord, grow and prosper according to your will, and in due time, let the promise of the reader be heard every time. Amen.

(Hebrews 4:16)

Wanted until Found

I want a man to fall in love with my mind.

Inspire my thoughts.

And explore my imagination.

I want him to feel close to my smile and enjoy my heartbeat.

I want him to grab my joy and reciprocate my peace.

Is this possible?

I say, yes, it is

Until then, I'm enjoying me.

Wanted until Found

INSIGHT

People tend to want what they want and want to have it when they want it. Romantic love is not as easy to come by, especially when already spending an insurmountable time in the wrong relationships. Remember the saying: Don't let your wants hurt you. What if this is true? As you yearn for that human experience that will make you smile, while you are waiting, smile and enjoy every good and wonderful thing that happens to you and for you. You must smile every day (even in your singleness). Smile because God woke you up. Smile because of God's mercy. Smile because you are covered by the blood of Jesus.

REFLECTION

- Have you ever wanted to be in a romantic relationship and was rejected?
- If so, did you try to change their mind about you?
- Will you still be okay if a romantic love never comes your way?

PRAYER

Dear God, we come to you frequently asking for blessings and favor. Lord God, I humbly ask that you bless the reader with the desires of their heart. Lord God, tie them to what is good. For we know that every good and perfect thing comes from you. Let the reader be satisfied in their season. Remind them that while they wait for romance, you are with them always, and can provide for them like no other. Amen.
(Philippians 4:19-20)

Who Are You Rolling With?

The pressure is on
The time has come
Who do you keep as your #1?

Will it be the one who rises the sun?
or the one who cares about none?

Will it be the one who loves you without condition?
or the one who tricks you into submission?

Will it be the one who deserves all glory?
or the one who is cunning and alluring?

Will it be the one who holds all power in His hand?
or the one who kills, steals, and destroys the land?

The one who you give the most attention to IS the one
you are rolling with.

Who Are You Rolling With?

INSIGHT

The enjoyment that the world offers will bring corruption to the spirit. The world makes the young look old, the weak look strong, and makes the sinner look like a saint. All tricks of the enemy! It is important to put on the full armor of God to deter the schemes, tactics, lies, and chaos from getting through to you. It is always best to reject, rebuke, or avoid the things meant to give you a hefty dose of regret. It is also important to choose salvation over persuasion. You must choose intelligently, because there is a heaven or hell waiting for you.

REFLECTION

- Are you enjoying the things of the world?
- How do the offerings of the world make you feel?
- If they make you feel bad, when will you confess and repent? (The answer is now.)

PRAYER

Prayer: Heavenly Father, giving all glory, honor, and praise to you in advance for the reader who is taking steps to be closer to you instead of stepping further away from you. Lord God, it is in Jesus' name that double-mindedness, uncertainty, fear, and indecisiveness is rebuked. Order the reader's steps, Lord, and send them a witness to assure them they are welcome to come back to You. Amen.

(1 John 2:15-17)

Yesterday

What yesterday meant to you
won't mean the same thing to me

because something in your yesterday may have given
you the blues...

For me, yesterday gave an opportunity too great to refuse

Your yesterday may have been bitter
like the taste of black coffee with no cream

My yesterday was exciting
because I've joined a winning team

Your yesterday hurt you and put a knot on your face
While yesterday for me felt comfy and safe

Your yesterday may leave you to question:

Should I go left or right or stay in-between
Should I run back to the things that hurt and sting
Should I allow that hit, kick, or punch
Or should I be brave and fight back for once
Should I stand up, talk up, or give a stare
Or do I share my concerns with God in prayer

Don't allow the happenings of your yesterday to fill you
with despair, or rob you of the desire to show others
you care

It would be quite sad to look for a blessing in your present day
because you could not see that the blessing already came in
your...

Yesterday

 *Yesterday*

INSIGHT

Whether you look at things with optimism or pessimism, there are consequences to both. Optimism encourages you and gives space to clear your mind and add to it the thoughts of hope, joy, peace, and love. Pessimism bogs your mind down and adds to it sadness, regret, depression, and despair. To avoid being pessimistic, connect with people who will affirm you. And more importantly, stay connected to God. Yesterday becomes a part of your past the moment a new day begins. Use it to learn. For when you don't, the lesson of yesterday will keep repeating itself.

REFLECTION

- What happened in your past that continues to have a negative impact on you?
- Have you addressed the people who hurt you with a written note, or have you had an intentional conversation with them?
- How we feel affects our health. Do you have anxiety, depression, or high blood pressure?
- When was the last time you had a spiritual checkup?

PRAYER

Heavenly Father, thank you! Thank you for showing the reader a new way to look at their circumstances. Lord God, free them from whatever has a hold on them. Protect and shield them,

Lord, from hurt, harm, and danger. Let them know that troubles won't last always. And, Lord, all praise belongs to you, for the grace and mercy that you give is sufficient. Amen. (Lamentations 3:22-23)

Dear Reader,

I thank you for taking time out of your day to read this collection of poems and insight. The takeaway in every poem or circumstance is that God is your strength, your healer, your provider, your friend. There is nothing you cannot overcome when you have God on your side. Trust in the Lord with all your heart. Everything you say and do will lead you to your destiny or destruction. I encourage you to learn to listen more and be slow to speak.

Why?

Because your words matter...

Happy reading, until the next book!

Thank you for reading *More than Just Poetry*
If you enjoyed this book or if you found it help-
ful to you or anyone in your life, please help spread
the word by leaving an online review. Thank you!

KEEP UP WITH YUMICA P. THOMPSON
Facebook: Yumica Thompson
Instagram: @yumicathompson
Twitter: @thompsonyumica

Made in the USA
Middletown, DE
19 March 2021